HERSHEY'S

Homemade ™

Over 100 recipes
for today's life-styles.

Hershey's. It's as rich in heritage as it is in great taste.

Milton S. Hershey began his chocolate enterprise in 1894, dedicating himself to producing only the finest milk chocolate products. This tradition has lived on for almost a century. Today, Hershey's remains devoted to providing you with the rich, quality chocolate you've come to know and trust. And that makes us "America's Chocolate Authority™."

Mr. Hershey's pioneering spirit and love of chocolate inspired him to build what was to become the world's largest chocolate factory in Hershey, PA. Now let the irresistible recipes in *Hershey's Homemade,* brought to you by your friends here in the Hershey Kitchens, inspire *you* to revive the wonderful tradition of baking mouth-watering desserts from scratch. Fill your kitchen with the enticing aroma of freshly baked cookies, pies, cakes and more. Create the rich taste chocolate lovers enjoy when you bake with quality Hershey's baking products.

Our experts here in the Kitchens developed and tested each of these delicious recipes, so please feel free to contact us with your questions or comments about them or any of our fine chocolate products. Write us at: The Hershey Kitchens, P.O. Box 815, Hershey, PA 17033-0815, or call our Consumer Relations Department toll-free, weekdays 9 a.m to 4 p.m., Eastern Time, 1-800-468-1714.

Discover all the tempting treats you can bake with everyone's favorite chocolate — Hershey's!

Sincerely,

The Hershey's Kitchens

CONTENTS

CAKES 4

CANDIES & SNACKS . . 50

DESSERTS 20

COOKIES 60

PIES 30

BROWNIES & BARS . . 72

CHEESECAKES 40

LIGHTER DESSERTS . . 84

INDEX 92

CAKES

The traditional family dessert. You'll love baking homemade goodness into these tried-and-true favorites, plus a variety of new temptations your family won't be able to resist. Enjoy creating sheet cakes, layer cakes and pound cakes, and topping them off with creamy, delicious frostings.

Triple Chocolate Torte (left), MINI CHIP Sour Cream Streusel Cake (right), recipes page 16.

Chocolate Bar Cake

This rich, moist chocolate cake is made special with the addition of the HERSHEY'S Milk Chocolate Bar.

1 HERSHEY'S Milk Chocolate Bar (7 oz.), broken into pieces
1/2 cup (1 stick) butter or margarine, softened
1 cup boiling water
2 cups all-purpose flour
1 1/2 cups sugar
1/2 cup HERSHEY'S Cocoa
2 teaspoons baking soda
1 teaspoon salt
2 eggs
1/2 cup dairy sour cream
1 teaspoon vanilla extract
VANILLA GLAZE (recipe follows)

Heat oven to 350°F. Grease and flour 12-cup fluted tube pan. In small bowl, stir together chocolate bar pieces, butter and water until chocolate is melted. In large mixer bowl, stir together flour, sugar, cocoa, baking soda and salt; gradually add chocolate mixture, beating until thoroughly blended. Add eggs, sour cream and vanilla; blend well. Beat on medium speed of electric mixer 1 minute. Pour batter into prepared pan. Bake 50 to 55 minutes or until wooden pick inserted in center comes out clean. Cool 10 minutes; remove from pan to wire rack. Cool completely. Drizzle VANILLA GLAZE over cake. *10 to 12 servings.*

VANILLA GLAZE: In medium microwave-safe bowl, place 1/4 cup (1/2 stick) butter or margarine. Microwave at HIGH (100%) 30 seconds or until melted. Gradually stir in 2 cups powdered sugar, 2 to 3 tablespoons hot water and 1 teaspoon vanilla extract; beat with wire whisk until smooth and slightly thickened. *About 1 1/4 cups glaze.*

Black Magic Cake

Mouthwateringly moist, with mysterious dark depths of flavor, this is our most requested cake recipe.

2 cups sugar
1 3/4 cups all-purpose flour
3/4 cup HERSHEY'S Cocoa
2 teaspoons baking soda
1 teaspoon baking powder
1 teaspoon salt
2 eggs
1 cup strong black coffee or 2 teaspoons powdered instant coffee plus 1 cup boiling water
1 cup buttermilk or sour milk*
1/2 cup vegetable oil
1 teaspoon vanilla extract

Heat oven to 350°F. Grease and flour two 9-inch round baking pans or one 13 × 9 × 2-inch baking pan. In large mixer bowl, blend sugar, flour, cocoa, baking soda, baking powder and salt. Add eggs, coffee, buttermilk, oil and vanilla; beat on medium speed of electric mixer 2 minutes (batter will be thin). Pour batter into prepared pan. Bake 30 to 35 minutes for round pans, 35 to 40 minutes for rectangular pan or until wooden pick inserted in center comes out clean. Cool 10 minutes; remove from pans to wire racks. Cool completely. Frost as desired. *10 to 12 servings.*

*To sour milk: Use 1 tablespoon white vinegar plus milk to equal 1 cup.

Top to Bottom: Chocolate Bar Cake, Black Magic Cake, recipes page 6; Dark Chocolate Pecan Torte, recipe page 8.

Dark Chocolate Pecan Torte

    4 squares (4 oz.) HERSHEY'S
       Unsweetened Baking
       Chocolate, broken into pieces
  1/3 cup butter or margarine
1 1/2 cups sugar
1 1/2 teaspoons vanilla extract
    3 eggs, separated
  1/2 cup all-purpose flour
    3 tablespoons water
  3/4 cup finely chopped pecans
  1/8 teaspoon cream of tartar
  1/8 teaspoon salt
       CHOCOLATE GLAZE (recipe
       follows)

In small microwave-safe bowl, place chocolate and butter. Microwave at HIGH (100%) 1 minute or until smooth when stirred; cool slightly. Line bottom of 9-inch springform pan with foil; butter foil and side of pan. Heat oven to 350°F. In large mixer bowl, combine chocolate mixture, sugar and vanilla; beat well. Add egg yolks, one at a time, beating well after each addition. Blend in flour and water; beat well. Stir in pecans. In small mixer bowl, beat egg whites, cream of tartar and salt until stiff peaks form; carefully fold into chocolate mixture. Pour batter into prepared pan. Bake 45 minutes or until top appears dry (torte will not test done in center). Cool 1 hour. Cover; refrigerate until firm. Remove side of pan. Invert onto serving plate; remove bottom of pan. Carefully remove foil. Pour CHOCOLATE GLAZE over torte; spread evenly on top and sides. *10 to 12 servings.*

CHOCOLATE GLAZE: In small mixer bowl, combine 1 cup powdered sugar and 1/2 teaspoon vanilla extract; set aside. In small microwave-safe bowl, place 2 tablespoons butter or margarine, 2 tablespoons water and 1 square (1 oz.) HERSHEY'S Unsweetened Baking Chocolate. Microwave at HIGH (100%) 1 minute or until smooth when stirred. Add to sugar mixture, beating until smooth. Add hot water, 1/2 teaspoon at a time, if needed for desired consistency.

Chocolate Chip Snack Cake

This snack cake also is a great coffee cake.

       FILLING (recipe follows)
    3 cups all-purpose flour
    2 cups sugar
  2/3 cup HERSHEY'S Cocoa
    2 teaspoons baking soda
    1 teaspoon salt
    2 cups water
  2/3 cup vegetable oil
    2 eggs
    2 tablespoons white vinegar
    2 teaspoons vanilla extract
    1 cup HERSHEY'S Semi-Sweet
       Chocolate Chips
  1/2 cup chopped nuts

Prepare FILLING; set aside. Heat oven to 350°F. Grease and flour bottom of 13 × 9 × 2-inch baking pan. In large mixer bowl, stir together flour, sugar, cocoa, baking soda and salt. Add water, oil, eggs, vinegar and vanilla; beat on medium speed of electric mixer 2 minutes or until well combined. Stir in chocolate chips. Pour batter into prepared pan. Spoon heaping teaspoonfuls FILLING evenly over batter. Sprinkle nuts over top. Bake 50 to 55 minutes or until wooden pick inserted in center comes out clean. Cool in pan on wire rack. Cover; store leftovers in refrigerator. *12 to 16 servings.*

FILLING

    1 package (8 oz.) cream cheese,
       softened
  1/3 cup sugar
    1 egg
  1/2 teaspoon vanilla extract
    1 cup HERSHEY'S Semi-Sweet
       Chocolate Chips

In small bowl, stir together cream cheese, sugar, egg and vanilla; beat until smooth. Stir in chocolate chips.

Hot Fudge Pudding Cake

Magically making its own fudge sauce, this cake will become one of your favorite last-minute desserts. Serve it with ice cream for an extra special treat.

1¼ cups granulated sugar, divided
1 cup all-purpose flour
7 tablespoons HERSHEY'S Cocoa, divided
2 teaspoons baking powder
¼ teaspoon salt
½ cup milk
⅓ cup butter or margarine, melted
1½ teaspoons vanilla extract
½ cup packed light brown sugar
1¼ cups hot water
    Whipped topping

Heat oven to 350°F. In medium bowl, stir together ¾ cup granulated sugar, flour, 3 tablespoons cocoa, baking powder and salt. Blend in milk, butter and vanilla; beat until smooth. Pour batter into 8- or 9-inch square baking pan. In separate bowl, stir together remaining ½ cup granulated sugar, brown sugar and remaining 4 tablespoons cocoa; sprinkle mixture evenly over batter. Pour hot water over top; do not stir. Bake 35 to 40 minutes or until center is almost set. Let stand 15 minutes; spoon into dessert dishes, spooning sauce from bottom of pan over top. Garnish with whipped topping. *About 8 servings.*

Old-Fashioned Chocolate Cake

¾ cup (1½ sticks) butter or margarine, softened
1⅔ cups sugar
3 eggs
1 teaspoon vanilla extract
2 cups all-purpose flour
⅔ cup HERSHEY'S Cocoa
1¼ teaspoons baking soda
1 teaspoon salt
¼ teaspoon baking powder
1⅓ cups water
    ONE-BOWL BUTTERCREAM FROSTING (recipe follows)

Heat oven to 350°F. Grease and flour two 9-inch round baking pans. In large mixer bowl, combine butter, sugar, eggs and vanilla; beat on high speed of electric mixer 3 minutes. In separate bowl, stir together flour, cocoa, baking soda, salt and baking powder; add alternately with water to butter mixture. Blend just until combined. Pour batter into prepared pans. Bake 30 to 35 minutes or until wooden pick inserted in center comes out clean. Cool 10 minutes; remove from pans to wire racks. Cool completely. Frost with ONE-BOWL BUTTERCREAM FROSTING. *8 to 10 servings.*

ONE-BOWL BUTTERCREAM FROSTING

6 tablespoons butter or margarine, softened
2⅔ cups powdered sugar
½ cup HERSHEY'S Cocoa
⅓ cup milk
1 teaspoon vanilla extract

In small mixer bowl, beat butter. Add powdered sugar and cocoa alternately with milk; beat to spreading consistency (additonal milk may be needed). Blend in vanilla. *About 2 cups frosting.*

Espresso Filled Mini Cakes

2 cups sugar
1³/4 cups all-purpose flour
³/4 cup HERSHEY'S Cocoa
1¹/2 teaspoons baking powder
1¹/2 teaspoons baking soda
1 teaspoon salt
2 eggs
1 cup milk
¹/2 cup vegetable oil
2 teaspoons vanilla extract
1 cup boiling water
ESPRESSO CREAM FILLING
(recipe follows) OR apricot
preserves or other flavor of
your choice
COCOA GLAZE (recipe
follows)

Heat oven to 350°F. Grease and lightly flour fourteen 6-ounce custard cups. In large mixer bowl, stir together sugar, flour, cocoa, baking powder, baking soda and salt. Add eggs, milk, oil and vanilla; beat on medium speed of electric mixer 2 minutes. Remove from mixer; stir in water (batter will be thin). Fill each prepared cup with scant ¹/2 cup batter. Place custard cups on cookie sheet. Bake 20 to 22 minutes or until wooden pick inserted in center comes out clean. Cool 5 minutes on wire racks; remove mini cakes from cups. Cool completely.

Espresso Filled Mini Cakes (top), recipe page 11; Old-Fashioned Chocolate Cake (bottom), recipe page 9.

Cut mini cakes horizontally about 1 inch from top. Spread bottom with FILLING or preserves; replace top of cake. Drizzle with COCOA GLAZE. Refrigerate until serving time. Refrigerate leftovers. *About 14 mini cakes.*

ESPRESSO CREAM FILLING: In small mixer bowl, combine 1 cup cold whipping cream, ¹/4 cup powdered sugar and 2 teaspoons powdered instant espresso; beat until stiff. *About 2 cups filling.*

COCOA GLAZE

¹/2 cup whipping cream
1¹/2 teaspoons light corn syrup
¹/2 cup HERSHEY'S Cocoa
¹/2 cup sugar
1 tablespoon butter
1¹/2 teaspoons vanilla extract

In small saucepan, stir together whipping cream and corn syrup. In bowl, stir together cocoa and sugar; add to cream mixture, stirring well. Add butter. Cook over low heat, stirring constantly, until butter melts and mixture is smooth. DO NOT BOIL. Remove from heat; stir in vanilla. Cool to desired consistency. *About 1 cup glaze.*

BAKER'S TIPS

Hershey's Cocoa is a favorite ingredient in recipes developed by the Hershey Kitchens. It is so convenient to use because it is easy to measure, can be used right from the can, blends easily with other ingredients and gives desserts a rich chocolate flavor. To use in your favorite recipe, use the simple method listed below:

To substitute cocoa for baking chocolate in recipes, use 3 level tablespoons HERSHEY'S Cocoa plus 1 tablespoon shortening or vegetable oil for 1 square (1 oz.) unsweetened baking chocolate.

To substitute for pre-melted chocolate, use 3 level tablespoons HERSHEY'S Cocoa plus 1 tablespoon melted shortening or vegetable oil for 1 envelope (1 oz.) pre-melted unsweetened chocolate.

MINI CHIP Angel Cake

1 **package (14.5 oz.) angel food cake mix**
1 **cup HERSHEY'S MINI CHIPS Semi-Sweet Chocolate**
  SATINY MINI CHIPS GLAZE (recipe follows) (optional)

Prepare cake mix as directed on package. Gently fold in small chocolate chips, distributing evenly. Pour batter into ungreased 10-inch tube pan; cut through batter several times with knife or spatula to loosen air bubbles. Bake as directed on package. Glaze with SATINY MINI CHIPS GLAZE, if desired. *10 to 12 servings.*

SATINY MINI CHIPS GLAZE: In small saucepan, heat 2 tablespoons sugar and 2 tablespoons water to boiling; stir until sugar dissolves. Remove from heat. Immediately add 1/2 cup HERSHEY'S MINI CHIPS Semi-Sweet Chocolate, stirring until melted. Continue stirring to desired consistency. *About 1/2 cup glaze.*

Left to Right: MINI CHIP Angel Cake, Double Chocolate Cocoa Cupcakes, recipes page 12; Feathery Fudge Cake, recipe page 13.

Double Chocolate Cocoa Cupcakes

1 1/4 **cups sugar**
  3/4 **cup shortening**
    2 **eggs**
    1 **teaspoon vanilla extract**
1 3/4 **cups all-purpose flour**
  1/2 **cup HERSHEY'S Cocoa**
    1 **teaspoon baking soda**
  1/2 **teaspoon salt**
    1 **cup milk**
    1 **cup HERSHEY'S MINI CHIPS Semi-Sweet Chocolate**
      Powdered sugar

Heat oven to 375°F. Paper-line 24 muffin cups (2 1/2 inches in diameter). In large mixer bowl, beat sugar and shortening until light and fluffy; beat in eggs and vanilla. In separate bowl, stir together flour, cocoa, baking soda and salt; add alternately with milk to beaten mixture. Beat thoroughly. Fold in small chocolate chips. Fill each muffin cup 3/4 full with batter. Bake 20 to 25 minutes or until cupcake springs back when touched lightly in center. Cool completely. Sprinkle powdered sugar over top of cupcakes. *About 2 dozen cupcakes.*

HERSHEY'S Disappearing Cake

We call this HERSHEY'S Disappearing Cake, because once you've made it, it disappears fast!

- 1/4 cup (1/2 stick) butter or margarine, softened
- 1/4 cup shortening
- 2 cups sugar
- 1 teaspoon vanilla extract
- 2 eggs
- 1 3/4 cups all-purpose flour
- 3/4 cup HERSHEY'S Cocoa
- 3/4 teaspoon baking powder
- 3/4 teaspoon baking soda
- 1/8 teaspoon salt
- 1 3/4 cups milk

Heat oven to 350°F. Grease and flour 13 × 9 × 2-inch baking pan. In large mixer bowl, beat butter, shortening, sugar and vanilla until light and fluffy. Add eggs; beat well. In separate bowl, stir together flour, cocoa, baking powder, baking soda and salt; add alternately with milk to butter mixture, blending well. Pour batter into prepared pan. Bake 35 to 40 minutes or until wooden pick inserted in center comes out clean. Cool in pan on wire rack. Frost as desired. *12 to 15 servings.*

Feathery Fudge Cake

- 2 1/2 squares (2 1/2 oz.) HERSHEY'S Unsweetened Baking Chocolate, broken into pieces
- 3/4 cup (1 1/2 sticks) butter or margarine, softened
- 2 cups sugar
- 1 teaspoon vanilla extract
- 2 eggs
- 2 1/4 cups all-purpose flour
- 1 1/4 teaspoons baking soda
- 1/2 teaspoon salt
- 1 1/3 cups water

Heat oven to 350°F. In small microwave-safe bowl, place chocolate. Microwave at HIGH (100%) 1 1/2 to 2 minutes or until smooth when stirred; set aside to cool slightly. Grease and flour two 9-inch round baking pans. In large mixer bowl, beat butter, sugar and vanilla until light and fluffy. Add eggs and cooled chocolate; blend well. In separate bowl, stir together flour, baking soda and salt; add alternately with water to butter mixture. Pour batter into prepared pans. Bake 35 to 40 minutes or until wooden pick inserted in center comes out clean. Cool 10 minutes; remove from pans to wire racks. Cool completely. Frost as desired. *10 to 12 servings.*

Chocolate Truffle Cake Supreme

The small amount of flour is not a mistake! This cake is similar to flourless chocolate cakes you may have had in restaurants.

1 1/4 cups (2 1/2 sticks) unsalted butter
3/4 cup HERSHEY'S Cocoa
1 cup plus 1 tablespoon sugar, divided
1 tablespoon all-purpose flour
2 teaspoons vanilla extract
4 eggs, separated
1 cup (1/2 pt.) cold whipping cream
Chocolate curls (optional)

Heat oven to 425°F. Grease bottom of 8-inch springform pan. In medium saucepan over low heat, melt butter. Add cocoa and 1 cup sugar, stirring until well blended. Remove from heat; cool slightly. Stir in flour and vanilla. Add egg yolks, one at a time, beating well after each addition. In small mixer bowl, beat egg whites with remaining 1 tablespoon sugar until soft peaks form; gradually fold into chocolate mixture. Spoon batter into prepared pan. Bake 16 to 18 minutes or until edges are firm (center will be soft). Cool completely on wire rack (cake will sink slightly in center as it cools). Remove rim of pan. Refrigerate cake at least 6 hours. In small mixer bowl, beat whipping cream until soft peaks form; spread over top of cake. Cut cake while cold, but let stand at room temperature 10 to 15 minutes before serving. Garnish with chocolate curls, if desired. *10 servings.*

Crater Cake

3 squares (3 oz.) HERSHEY'S Unsweetened Baking Chocolate, broken into pieces
1/3 cup butter or margarine
1 3/4 cups all-purpose flour
1 1/2 cups sugar
1 1/2 teaspoons baking soda
1 teaspoon salt
1 1/2 cups (12 oz.) dairy sour cream
2 eggs
1 teaspoon vanilla extract
1/2 cup chopped nuts

Prepare CHOCOLATE TOPPING; set aside. Heat oven to 350°F. Grease and flour 13 × 9 × 2-inch baking pan. In small microwave-safe bowl, place chocolate and butter. Microwave at HIGH (100%) 2 to 2 1/2 minutes or until melted when stirred; cool slightly. In large mixer bowl, combine cooled chocolate, flour, sugar, baking soda, salt, sour cream, eggs and vanilla. Blend on low speed of electric mixer. Beat on medium speed 3 minutes until smooth. Pour batter into prepared pan. Top with 1/2 teaspoonfuls CHOCOLATE TOPPING about 1 inch apart over batter. With fork, gently streak mounds over batter for marbled effect. Sprinkle with nuts. Bake 35 to 40 minutes or until wooden pick inserted in cake (not craters) comes out clean. Cool completely in pan on wire rack. *12 to 15 servings.*

CHOCOLATE TOPPING

1 square (1 oz.) HERSHEY'S Unsweetened Baking Chocolate, broken into pieces
1 tablespoon butter or margarine
3/4 cup powdered sugar
2 tablespoons milk
1/4 teaspoon vanilla extract

In small microwave-safe bowl, place chocolate and butter. Microwave at HIGH (100%) 1 minute or until smooth when stirred; cool slightly. In small mixer bowl, beat powdered sugar, milk and vanilla until smooth. Add chocolate mixture; beat on high speed 2 minutes. Set aside.

Chocolate Raspberry Pound Cake

Dark and luscious, this cake is bursting with chocolate and raspberry flavors.

1   cup seedless black raspberry
    preserves, divided*
2   cups all-purpose flour
1 1/2 cups sugar
3/4 cup HERSHEY'S Cocoa
1 1/2 teaspoons baking soda
1   teaspoon salt
2/3 cup butter or margarine,
    softened
2   cups (16 oz.) dairy sour cream
2   eggs
1   teaspoon vanilla extract
    Powdered sugar
    RASPBERRY CREAM (recipe
    follows)

Heat oven to 350°F. Grease and flour 12-cup fluted tube pan. In small microwave-safe bowl, place 3/4 cup preserves. Microwave at HIGH (100%) 30 to 45 seconds or until melted; cool. In large mixer bowl, stir together flour, sugar, cocoa, baking soda and salt. Add butter, sour cream, eggs, vanilla and melted preserves; beat on medium speed of electric mixer 3 to 4 minutes or until well blended. Pour batter into prepared pan. Bake 50 to 60 minutes or until wooden pick inserted in center comes out clean. Cool 10 minutes; remove from pan to wire rack. In small microwave-safe bowl, place remaining 1/4 cup preserves. Microwave at HIGH 30 seconds or until melted; brush over warm cake. Cool completely. At serving time, sprinkle powdered sugar over top. Fill cake cavity with RASPBERRY CREAM. *About 12 servings.*

*Red raspberry jam may be substituted.

RASPBERRY CREAM: Thaw 1 package (10 oz.) frozen red raspberries in light syrup. Purée in food processor or blender. In medium bowl, strain to remove seeds; discard seeds. Blend 1 container (8 oz.) frozen non-dairy whipped topping, thawed, with raspberry purée. Stir in 2 tablespoons Chambord (raspberry-flavored liqueur), if desired.

15

Triple Chocolate Torte

For true chocolate lovers, this chocolate masterpiece will become one of your favorite recipes. We like to top it off with chocolate curls.

  2 eggs, separated
1 1/2 cups sugar, divided
1 1/4 cups all-purpose flour
  1/2 cup HERSHEY'S Cocoa
  3/4 teaspoon baking soda
  1/2 teaspoon salt
  1/2 cup vegetable oil
  1 cup buttermilk or sour milk*
    CHOCOLATE CREAM FILLING
    (recipe follows)
    CHOCOLATE GLAZE (recipe
    page 18)

Heat oven to 350°F. Grease and flour two 9-inch round baking pans. In small mixer bowl, beat egg whites until foamy; gradually beat in 1/2 cup sugar until stiff peaks form. In large mixer bowl, stir together remaining 1 cup sugar, flour, cocoa, baking soda and salt. Add oil, buttermilk and egg yolks; beat until smooth. Gently fold egg whites into batter. Pour batter into prepared pans. Bake 25 to 30 minutes or until cake springs back when touched lightly in center. Cool 5 minutes; remove from pans to wire racks. Cool completely. Split layers in half horizontally. Prepare CHOCOLATE CREAM FILLING. Spread cake layer with 1/3 cream filling; top with second cake layer. Repeat procedure ending with plain layer on top. Prepare CHOCOLATE GLAZE; glaze cake. Refrigerate; store leftovers in refrigerator.
8 to 10 servings.

*To sour milk: Use 1 tablespoon white vinegar plus milk to equal 1 cup.

CHOCOLATE CREAM FILLING: In small mixer bowl, combine 2/3 cup sugar and 1/3 cup HERSHEY'S Cocoa. Add 1 1/2 cups cold whipping cream and 1 1/2 teaspoons vanilla extract; beat on low speed of electric mixer to combine. Beat on medium speed until stiff.

MINI CHIP Sour Cream Streusel Cake

  3/4 cup (1 1/2 sticks) margarine,
    softened
1 1/2 cups sugar
  3 eggs
  1 teaspoon vanilla extract
  3 cups all-purpose flour
1 1/2 teaspoons baking powder
1 1/2 teaspoons baking soda
  1/4 teaspoon salt
1 1/2 cups (12 oz.) dairy sour cream
1 1/2 cups HERSHEY'S MINI CHIPS
    Semi-Sweet Chocolate
  1/4 cup packed light brown sugar
  1/4 cup finely chopped nuts
  1/2 teaspoon ground cinnamon
    SATINY MINI CHIP GLAZE
    (recipe follows)

Heat oven to 350°F. Grease 12-cup fluted tube pan. In large mixer bowl, beat margarine, sugar, eggs and vanilla until light and fluffy. In separate bowl, stir together flour, baking powder, baking soda and salt; add alternately with sour cream to margarine mixture. Stir in small chocolate chips. Spread half of batter in prepared pan. In small bowl, combine brown sugar, nuts and cinnamon; sprinkle evenly over batter. Spread remaining batter evenly over top. Bake 55 to 60 minutes or until golden brown and wooden pick inserted in cake comes out clean. Cool 15 minutes; remove from pan to wire rack. Cool completely. Glaze with SATINY MINI CHIPS GLAZE.
10 servings.

SATINY MINI CHIPS GLAZE: In small saucepan, heat 2 tablespoons sugar and 2 tablespoons water to boiling; stir until sugar dissolves. Remove from heat. Immediately add 1/2 cup HERSHEY'S MINI CHIPS Semi-Sweet Chocolate, stirring until melted. Continue stirring to desired consistency. *About 1/2 cup glaze.*

Montana Mountain Cake

High as a Montana mountain, this three-layered beauty will impress your family.

 1 **cup (2 sticks) butter or margarine, softened**
 2 **cups sugar**
 3 **eggs**
 1 1/2 **teaspoons vanilla extract**
 2 1/2 **cups all-purpose flour**
 1/2 **cup HERSHEY'S Cocoa**
 1 1/2 **teaspoons baking soda**
 1/2 **teaspoon salt**
 1 1/2 **cups ice water**
 MOUNTAIN MOCHA FROSTING (recipe follows)

Heat oven to 375°F. Grease and flour three 8- or 9-inch round baking pans. In large mixer bowl, beat butter and sugar until creamy. Add eggs, one at a time, beating well after each addition; beat 2 additional minutes. Add vanilla. In separate bowl, stir together flour, cocoa, baking soda and salt; add alternately with water to butter mixture, beating until blended. Divide batter evenly among prepared pans. Spread batter to edges of pans and slightly up sides. Bake 25 to 30 minutes or until cake begins to pull away from sides of pans. Cool 5 minutes; remove from pans to wire racks. Cool completely. Fill and frost layers with MOUNTAIN MOCHA FROSTING. *10 to 12 servings.*

MOUNTAIN MOCHA FROSTING

 4 **egg whites**
 1 **cup packed light brown sugar**
 1 **tablespoon powdered instant coffee dissolved in 1/4 cup hot water**
 1 **teaspoon cream of tartar**
 1/8 **teaspoon salt**
 1 1/2 **teaspoons vanilla extract**

In top of double boiler, combine egg whites, brown sugar, coffee, cream of tartar and salt. Beat with hand-held electric mixer on low speed 30 seconds. Place over boiling water (upper pan should not touch water). Cook, beating constantly on high speed of electric mixer, 5 to 8 minutes or until mixture stands in peaks when beaters are removed. Remove from heat. Immediately spoon mixture into large bowl; add vanilla. Continue to beat on high speed 2 to 3 minutes to spreading consistency. *About 5 cups frosting.*

BAKER'S TIP

Chocolate curls make an especially festive garnish for cakes and other desserts and they are not difficult to make. The secret is to have chocolate at the proper temperature. It should be slightly warm but still firm. HERSHEY'S Unsweetened Baking Chocolate or a large HERSHEY'S Milk Chocolate Bar will work just fine. Place an unwrapped bar in a microwave oven at HIGH for about 30 seconds or just until chocolate feels slightly warm (or place on cookie sheet in oven that is only slightly warm). With even pressure, draw a vegetable peeler along the flat or underside of the chocolate. A curl will form. Carefully lift curl with a wooden pick onto a wax paper-covered tray. Refrigerate until firm. These curls can be kept refrigerated in a covered container for future use.

Quick Chocolate Fudge Frosting

2/3 cup butter or margarine
1¹/3 cups HERSHEY'S Cocoa or
   HERSHEY'S Premium
   European Style Cocoa
5¹/3 cups powdered sugar
2/3 cup milk
2 teaspoons vanilla extract

In medium saucepan, over medium heat, melt butter; add cocoa. Cook over medium heat, stirring constantly, until mixture thickens. Remove from heat. Spoon mixture into large mixer bowl; cool completely. Add powdered sugar alternately with milk, beating to spreading consistency. Blend in vanilla. *About 3¹/2 cups frosting.*

Note: 3¹/2 cups frosting will fill and frost an 8- or 9-inch two- or three-layer cake.

HERSHEY'S Chocolate Frosting

2 cups (12-oz. package)
   HERSHEY'S Semi-Sweet
   Chocolate Chips
2 cups powdered sugar
2/3 cup evaporated milk

In small microwave-safe bowl, place chocolate chips. Microwave at HIGH (100%) 1¹/2 minutes; stir. Microwave at HIGH additional 30 seconds or until melted and smooth when stirred. Gradually add powdered sugar and evaporated milk, beating until smooth. *About 2¹/2 cups frosting.*

One-Bowl Buttercream Frosting

This is an all-time favorite frosting for cakes, cupcakes or any frosting needs.

6 tablespoons butter or
   margarine, softened
2²/3 cups powdered sugar
   HERSHEY'S Cocoa or
   HERSHEY'S Premium
   European Style Cocoa
   light flavor — ¹/3 cup
   medium flavor — ¹/2 cup
   dark flavor — ³/4 cup
4 to 6 tablespoons milk
1 teaspoon vanilla extract

In small mixer bowl, beat butter. Add powdered sugar and cocoa alternately with milk; beat to spreading consistency. Blend in vanilla. *About 2 cups frosting.*

Chocolate Glaze

3 tablespoons butter or margarine
3 tablespoons light corn syrup
1 tablespoon water
1 cup HERSHEY'S Semi-Sweet
   Chocolate Chips

In small saucepan, combine butter, corn syrup and water; place over medium heat, stirring constantly, until mixture begins to boil. Remove from heat; stir in chocolate chips until melted. Cool to room temperature. *About 1 cup frosting.*

One-Bowl Buttercream Frosting (left), recipe page 18; Lemony Vanilla Milk Chip Frosting (right), recipe page 19.

18

Chocolate Cream Cheese Frosting

2 1/2 squares (2 1/2 oz.) HERSHEY'S
    Unsweetened Baking
    Chocolate, broken into pieces
1 package (3 oz.) cream cheese
1/4 cup milk
3 to 3 1/2 cups powdered sugar

In medium microwave-safe bowl, place chocolate, cream cheese and milk. Microwave at HIGH (100%) 1 1/2 minutes; stir. Microwave at HIGH an additional 30 seconds to 1 minute or until soft and smooth when stirred. Gradually add powdered sugar, beating until smooth. *About 2 cups frosting.*

Lemony Vanilla Milk Chip Frosting

1 2/3 cups (10-oz. package)
    HERSHEY'S Vanilla Milk Chips
1/2 cup whipping cream
1 1/4 to 1 1/2 cups powdered sugar
1 tablespoon freshly grated
    lemon peel
1 teaspoon lemon juice

In large microwave-safe bowl, place vanilla chips and whipping cream. Microwave at HIGH (100%) 30 seconds; stir vigorously. If necessary, microwave at HIGH an additional 15 seconds at a time, stirring vigorously after each heating, just until chips are melted when stirred. With wire whisk, gradually blend in powdered sugar, lemon peel and lemon juice. Stir until smooth and well blended. Refrigerate, if needed, for spreading consistency. *About 2 cups frosting.*

DESSERTS

An elegant rich dessert makes a pleasurable, beautiful ending to any great meal. Experiment with mousses and sauces while enjoying the silky-smooth satisfaction you only get when you bake with rich Hershey's chocolate. Then delight in tempting your guests with chocolately after-dinner treats when you entertain at home . . . or have volunteered to bring the dessert!

Choco-Berry Bavarian Cream (left), Pears with Chocolate-Orange Sauce (right), recipes page 22.

Pears with Chocolate-Orange Sauce

A simple, yet elegant, dessert.

6 fresh pears
1½ cups apple juice
1 teaspoon vanilla extract
CHOCOLATE-ORANGE SAUCE (recipe follows)

Slice piece off bottom of pears to make a flat base. Peel pears and core from bottom but leave stems intact. In large saucepan, combine juice with vanilla; add pears, base side down. Heat to boiling. Reduce heat; simmer covered, spooning juice over pears occasionally, 20 to 25 minutes or until pears are tender. Meanwhile, prepare CHOCOLATE-ORANGE SAUCE. To serve, place pear base side down in serving dish; spoon about 1 tablespoon warm sauce over top. *6 servings.*

CHOCOLATE-ORANGE SAUCE

¾ cup HERSHEY'S PREMIUM Semi-Sweet Chocolate Chunks
1 tablespoon vegetable shortening
¼ teaspoon orange extract

In medium microwave-safe bowl, place all ingredients. Microwave at HIGH (100%) 1½ to 2 minutes or until smooth when stirred. Serve warm sauce over hot poached pears. *About ½ cup sauce.*

BAKER'S TIP

HERSHEY'S European Style Cocoa is a "Dutched" Cocoa. Dutching is a process that neutralizes the natural acidity found in cocoa powder. This results in a darker cocoa with a more mellow chocolate flavor than HERSHEY'S Regular Cocoa.

Choco-Berry Bavarian Cream

Named for the Bavarian area in Germany, a classic Bavarian cream uses gelatin and whipped cream to achieve a richly flavored, light-textured dessert. This version also uses strawberries.

1 package (10 oz.) frozen strawberries in syrup, thawed OR 1 cup sweetened sliced fresh strawberries
2 envelopes unflavored gelatin
½ cup sugar
1 cup HERSHEY'S MINI CHIPS Semi-Sweet Chocolate
2¼ cups milk, divided
1 teaspoon vanilla extract
1 cup (½ pt.) cold whipping cream
STRAWBERRY CREAM (recipe follows)
Fresh strawberries (optional)

Drain strawberries; reserve syrup. Add water to syrup to equal ¾ cup. Sprinkle gelatin over liquid; set aside. Refrigerate drained berries. In medium saucepan, stir together sugar, small chocolate chips and ½ cup milk. Cook over low heat, stirring constantly, until mixture is smooth and very hot. Add gelatin mixture, stirring until gelatin is completely dissolved. Remove from heat; add remaining milk and vanilla. Pour into bowl; refrigerate, stirring occasionally, until mixture mounds when dropped from spoon. In small bowl, beat whipping cream until stiff; fold into chocolate mixture. Pour into oiled 5- or 6-cup mold; refrigerate until firm. Unmold; garnish with STRAWBERRY CREAM and fresh strawberries, if desired. *8 to 10 servings.*

STRAWBERRY CREAM: Mash or purée reserved strawberries from BAVARIAN CREAM recipe to equal ½ cup. In small mixer bowl, beat 1 cup (½ pt.) cold whipping cream and 1 teaspoon vanilla extract until stiff. Fold in strawberry purée and 2 to 3 drops red food color. *About 2 cups topping.*

Milk Chocolate Pots de Crème (top), Orange-Chocolate Mousse (bottom).

Orange-Chocolate Mousse

- 1 teaspoon unflavored gelatin
- 2 tablespoons cold water
- 1/2 cup sugar
- 1/4 cup HERSHEY'S Premium European Style Cocoa or HERSHEY'S Cocoa
- 1/4 cup water
- 2 tablespoons milk
- 1 teaspoon vanilla extract
- 1 cup (1/2 pt.) cold whipping cream
- 1/4 teaspoon freshly grated orange peel

In custard cup, sprinkle gelatin over cold water; let stand 1 minute. In small saucepan, combine sugar, cocoa and water; cook over low heat, stirring constantly, until hot and slightly thickened. Remove from heat; add softened gelatin, stirring until dissolved. Blend in milk and vanilla; cool. In small mixer bowl, combine whipping cream and orange peel; beat until stiff. Gradually add chocolate mixture to whipped cream. Spoon into dessert dishes; refrigerate at least 1 hour. *4 to 6 servings.*

Milk Chocolate Pots de Crème

- 2 cups (11.5-oz. package) HERSHEY'S Milk Chocolate Chips
- 1/2 cup light cream
- 1/2 teaspoon vanilla extract SWEETENED WHIPPED CREAM (recipe follows)

In medium microwave-safe bowl, place milk chocolate chips and light cream. Microwave at HIGH (100%) 1 1/2 minutes; stir. If necessary, microwave at HIGH an additional 15 seconds at a time, stirring after each heating, until chocolate is melted and mixture is smooth when stirred. Stir in vanilla. Pour into demitasse cups or very small soufflé dishes. Cover; refrigerate until firm. Serve cold with SWEETENED WHIPPED CREAM. *6 to 8 servings.*

SWEETENED WHIPPED CREAM:
In small mixer bowl, beat 1/2 cup cold whipping cream, 1 tablespoon powdered sugar and 1/2 teaspoon vanilla extract until stiff. Refrigerate until ready to serve. *About 1 cup whipped cream.*

Mocha-Filled Cream Puffs

1/2 cup water
1/4 cup (1/2 stick) butter or
    margarine
1/2 cup all-purpose flour
2 eggs
    MOCHA CREAM FILLING
    (recipe follows)
    Powdered sugar

Heat oven to 400°F. Grease cookie sheet. In medium saucepan, heat water and butter to rolling boil. Add flour all at once; stir vigorously over low heat about 1 minute or until mixture leaves side of pan and forms a ball. Remove from heat. Add eggs, one at a time, beating with spoon after each addition until smooth. Drop batter by scant 1/4 cupfuls about 3 inches apart onto prepared sheet. Bake 35 to 40 minutes or until golden brown. Remove from oven. Slice small portion from top of puffs; set aside. Remove any soft dough from inside of puffs. Remove from sheet to wire rack; cool completely. Prepare MOCHA CREAM FILLING; fill puffs. Replace tops; sprinkle with powdered sugar. Refrigerate until cold.
6 cream puffs.

MOCHA CREAM FILLING

2/3 cup sugar
3 tablespoons HERSHEY'S Cocoa
3 tablespoons cornstarch
1 1/2 cups milk
2 to 3 teaspoons powdered
    instant coffee
1 egg yolk, slightly beaten
1 tablespoon butter or
    margarine
1/2 teaspoon vanilla extract

In medium saucepan, stir together sugar, cocoa and cornstarch; stir in milk and instant coffee. Cook, stirring constantly, until mixture boils; boil and stir 1 minute. Remove from heat. Gradually stir small amount of hot mixture into egg yolk, blending well; return to pan. Stir and heat just to boiling. Remove from heat; stir in butter and vanilla. Pour into bowl; press plastic wrap onto surface. Refrigerate.

Vanilla Chip Fruit Tart

3/4 cup (1 1/2 sticks) butter or
    margarine, softened
1/2 cup powdered sugar
1 1/2 cups all-purpose flour
    VANILLA FILLING (recipe
    follows)
    FRUIT TOPPING (recipe
    follows)

Heat oven to 300°F. In small mixer bowl, beat butter and powdered sugar until smooth; blend in flour. Press mixture onto bottom and up side of 12-inch round pizza pan. Flute edge, if desired. Bake 20 to 25 minutes or until lightly browned; cool completely. Prepare VANILLA FILLING; spread on crust. Cover; refrigerate. Prepare FRUIT TOPPING. Cover; refrigerate assembled tart until just before serving. *10 to 12 servings.*

VANILLA FILLING: In microwave-safe bowl, place 1 2/3 cups (10-oz. package) HERSHEY'S Vanilla Milk Chips and 1/4 cup whipping cream. Microwave at HIGH (100%) 1 to 1 1/2 minutes or until chips are melted and mixture is smooth when stirred vigorously. Beat in 1 package (8 oz.) softened cream cheese.

FRUIT TOPPING

1/4 cup sugar
1 tablespoon cornstarch
1/2 cup pineapple juice
1/2 teaspoon lemon juice
    Assorted fresh fruit, sliced

In small saucepan, stir together sugar and cornstarch; stir in juices. Cook over medium heat, stirring constantly, until thickened; cool. Meanwhile, arrange fruit on top of filling; carefully pour or brush juice mixture over fruit.

Mocha-Filled Cream Puffs (top), Vanilla Chip Fruit Tart (bottom), recipes page 24.

Peanut Butter Washington Squares

This is a true old-fashioned comfort dessert made new with the addition of peanut butter chips.

1²/₃ cups (10-oz. package) REESE'S Peanut Butter Chips
¹/₂ cup (1 stick) margarine
1 cup sugar
2 eggs
2 teaspoons vanilla extract
2 cups all-purpose flour
1¹/₂ teaspoons baking soda
¹/₂ teaspoon salt
1 can (21 oz.) cherry pie filling (or any other fruit flavor pie filling)
Vanilla ice cream

Heat oven to 375°F. In microwave-safe bowl, place peanut butter chips. Microwave at HIGH (100%) 1 minute; stir. If necessary, microwave at HIGH an additional 15 seconds at a time, stirring after each heating, just until chips are melted when stirred. In large mixer bowl, beat margarine and sugar until light and fluffy. Add eggs and vanilla; beat well. Blend in melted chips. In separate bowl, stir together flour, baking soda and salt; add to margarine mixture. Divide dough in half. Press one half onto bottom of ungreased 13 × 9 × 2-inch baking pan. Bake 10 minutes; set aside to cool. Meanwhile, cover and refrigerate remaining dough until stiff enough to handle, about 30 minutes. Pour pie filling evenly over baked layer. Roll remaining dough between 2 pieces of wax paper to form a ¹/₄-inch-thick rectangle, 13 × 9 inches; cut into ¹/₂ × 13-inch strips. Lay strips, ¹/₂ inch apart, lattice-fashion, over pie filling in pan.* Bake 20 to 25 minutes or until browned. Serve warm with scoops of ice cream. *About 12 servings.*

* Broken strips of dough may be pieced together and will mesh during baking.

Chocolate-Banana Freeze

1   **envelope unflavored gelatin**
$1/2$ **cup cold water**
$1/3$ **cup sugar**
$1/4$ **cup HERSHEY'S Cocoa**
1   **cup very ripe mashed banana (2 medium bananas)**
1   **container (8 oz.) vanilla yogurt**
1   **cup frozen non-dairy whipped topping, thawed**

In small saucepan, sprinkle gelatin over water; let stand 2 minutes to soften. Stir in sugar and cocoa. Cook over low heat, stirring constantly, until gelatin is dissolved. Remove from heat; cool slightly. In medium bowl, stir together mashed banana and yogurt; blend in gelatin mixture. Fold in whipped topping. Spoon mixture into six 5-ounce paper cups; freeze partially. Insert wooden popsicle sticks; freeze until firm. To serve, peel off paper cup. *6 servings.*

Note: Mixture can be poured into foil-lined $7^3/8 \times 3^5/8 \times 2^1/4$-inch loaf pan; freeze until firm. Remove from pan; peel off foil. Cut into slices; garnish with thin banana slices, if desired. *10 servings.*

Choco-Berry Freeze

Try this the next time you want a summery, refreshing dessert.

1   **cup orange juice**
2   **cups strawberries, sliced**
$1/2$ **cup sugar**
$1/4$ **cup HERSHEY'S Cocoa**
1   **cup ($1/2$ pt.) cold whipping cream**

In blender, place orange juice and strawberries; cover and blend. Add remaining ingredients; blend until thoroughly combined. Pour mixture into cold 9-inch square pan. Freeze until hard around edges. Into blender, spoon semi-frozen mixture; blend until smooth. Pour mixture into 1-quart mold or return to square pan; cover and freeze until firm, 4 to 6 hours. To serve, unmold onto cold plate; cut into slices or spoon into dessert dishes. *About 8 servings.*

Left to Right: Chocolate-Banana Freeze, Choco-Berry Freeze.

Fudgey Chocolate Cherry Cups (top), Cocoa Creme with Apricot Sauce (bottom), recipes page 29.

Brandied Chocolate Sauce

Serve this rich brandy-flavored chocolate sauce over fruit, ice cream or pound cake.

- **6 tablespoons butter or margarine**
- **6 tablespoons HERSHEY'S Cocoa**
- **1 can (14 oz.) sweetened condensed milk**
- **1 1/2 teaspoons brandy extract or 3 tablespoons brandy**

In heavy saucepan over medium heat, melt butter. Remove from heat; add cocoa, stirring until smooth. Blend in sweetened condensed milk; return to heat, stirring constantly, until slightly thickened. Remove from heat; stir in brandy extract. If sauce becomes too thick add small amount of water. Serve as desired on fruit, cake or ice cream. *About 1 1/2 cups sauce.*

28

Fudgey Chocolate Cherry Cups

2/3 cup sugar
1/4 cup HERSHEY'S Premium
    European Style Cocoa
1 cup (1/2 pt.) light cream
3 tablespoons butter or
    margarine
3 egg yolks
2 tablespoons brandy or 3/4
    teaspoon brandy extract
1/4 teaspoon vanilla extract
12 maraschino cherries, cut into
    quarters
    Whipped cream (optional)
6 maraschino cherries (optional)

Heat oven to 325°F. In medium sauce-pan, stir together sugar and cocoa. Gradually stir in light cream; add butter. Cook over medium heat, stirring con-stantly, until mixture is hot and smooth. In medium bowl, lightly beat egg yolks; slowly whisk in cocoa mixture. Stir in brandy and vanilla extract. Place cut cherries in bottom of six small soufflé dishes. Place dishes in shallow baking pan; pour cocoa mixture into dishes. Place pan on rack in oven; pour about 1 inch hot water into pan. Bake 40 minutes. Remove dishes from pan. Cool to room temperature. Cover; re-frigerate 2 to 3 hours. (May be refrig-erated, well covered, up to 2 days.) Garnish with whipped cream and mar-aschino cherry, if desired. *6 servings.*

Note: One 9-inch pie plate may be substituted for small dishes. Bake as directed for 25 minutes. To serve, spoon small spoonfuls into small dessert dishes.

Cocoa Creme with Apricot Sauce

1 envelope unflavored gelatin
3/4 cup sugar
1/3 cup HERSHEY'S Cocoa
2 cups (1 pt.) whipping cream,
    divided
1 teaspoon vanilla extract
1 cup (8 oz.) dairy sour cream,
    divided
    APRICOT SAUCE (recipe
    follows)
    WHIPPED CREAM TOPPING
    (recipe follows)

In medium saucepan, mix gelatin with sugar; add cocoa. Blend in 1 1/2 cups whipping cream; let stand 1 minute. Cook over low heat, stirring constantly with wire whisk, until gelatin is com-pletely dissolved, about 5 minutes. Re-move from heat; stir in vanilla. Pour into medium bowl; cool to room temperature, stirring occasionally. With wire whisk, blend in 3/4 cup sour cream. Pour mixture into six custard cups or decorative molds. Refrigerate until set, about 3 hours. For each serv-ing, spoon about 1 tablespoon APRI-COT SAUCE on dessert plate. Unmold chocolate dessert onto sauce. Garnish with remaining sauce and WHIPPED CREAM TOPPING. *6 servings.*

APRICOT SAUCE: Drain 1 can (16 oz.) apricot halves in light syrup, reserving 3 tablespoons syrup. In food proces-sor bowl, place drained apricot halves, reserved syrup and 1 tablespoon apri-cot brandy*; process until smooth. Re-frigerate. *About 1 cup sauce.*

*1/4 teaspoon almond extract and 1/4 teaspoon grated lemon rind may be substituted for brandy.

WHIPPED CREAM TOPPING: In small mixer bowl, beat remaining 1/2 cup whip-ping cream and 2 tablespoons powdered sugar until stiff. Fold in remaining 1/4 cup sour cream. Refrigerate until serving time. *About 1 1/4 cups topping.*

PIES

These tasteful recipes inspire you to revive the time-honored art of scratch baking and give you the delectable homemade taste your family loves. Prepare flavorful crusts and fill them with rich chocolate and creamy peanut butter variations.

Festive Frozen Peanut Butter Pecan Pie (left), recipe page 34; Three-in-One Chocolate Pudding Pie (right), recipe page 38.

Celebration Tarts

These individual chocolate cherry tarts make a delicious finale to a meal.

Pastry dough for double crust 9-inch pie
1/3 **cup HERSHEY'S Cocoa**
1/3 **cup sugar**
3 **tablespoons water**
2 **tablespoons butter or margarine**
1 **can (21 oz.) cherry pie filling**
1 **egg**
2 **tablespoons light corn syrup**
1 **tablespoon packed light brown sugar**
1 **tablespoon butter or margarine, melted**
1 **cup coarsely chopped pecans**
Sweetened whipped cream

Place cookie sheet in oven; heat oven to 375°F. Roll out pastry on lightly floured surface. Cut out 6 circles about 5¾ inches in diameter, rerolling scraps as needed to make 6 circles. Press pastry circles evenly into 4¾-inch tart pans with removable bottoms, allowing pastry to extend ¼ inch above edges of pans; set aside. In small saucepan, stir together cocoa, sugar and water; add 2 tablespoons butter. Cook over low heat, stirring constantly with wire whisk, until butter melts and mixture is smooth. Cool to room temperature, about 10 minutes. Spread cocoa mixture on bottom of tart shells, dividing evenly. Spoon pie filling over mixture, dividing evenly. In small bowl, stir together egg, corn syrup, brown sugar and melted butter; stir in pecans. Spoon over pie filling, dividing equally. Place tart pans on preheated cookie sheet. Bake 30 minutes or until set and filling is bubbly. Cool completely in pans on wire rack. Remove tarts from pans. Garnish with whipped cream. *6 servings.*

Chocolate Marble Cheesepie

Make this no-bake cheesepie the next time you don't want to heat your oven.

CHOCOLATE CRUMB CRUST (recipe follows)
1/4 **cup HERSHEY'S Cocoa**
1 **can (14 oz.) sweetened condensed milk, divided**
3 **teaspoons vanilla extract, divided**
4 **packages (3 oz. each) cream cheese, softened**
2 **tablespoons lemon juice**
Chocolate curls (optional)

Prepare CHOCOLATE CRUMB CRUST. In small saucepan, stir together cocoa and ⅔ cup sweetened condensed milk. Cook over low heat, stirring constantly, until mixture is smooth and very thick. Remove from heat; stir in 1 teaspoon vanilla. In small mixer bowl, beat 2 packages cream cheese until light and fluffy; add cocoa mixture. Cool thoroughly. In large mixer bowl, beat remaining 2 packages cream cheese until light and fluffy. Gradually beat in remaining sweetened condensed milk, lemon juice and remaining 2 teaspoons vanilla. Alternately spoon vanilla and chocolate mixtures into prepared crust; gently swirl with knife or spatula for marbled effect. Refrigerate 8 hours or until firm. Garnish with chocolate curls, if desired. *6 to 8 servings.*

CHOCOLATE CRUMB CRUST:
In medium bowl, stir together 1¼ cups graham cracker crumbs, ¼ cup HERSHEY'S Cocoa and ¼ cup sugar. Blend in 6 tablespoons melted butter or margarine. Press mixture firmly on bottom and up sides of 9-inch pie plate; refrigerate about 2 hours before filling.

Chocolate Marble Cheesepie (top), Celebration Tarts (bottom).

Festive Frozen Peanut Butter Pecan Pie

1   cup broken pecans
1 1/2   tablespoons butter or margarine
1 2/3   cups (10-oz. package) REESE'S Peanut Butter Chips
1/2   cup milk
2   packages (3 oz.) cream cheese, softened
2/3   cup powdered sugar
1   envelope (1.3 oz.) whipped topping mix
   8-inch (6 oz.) packaged crumb crust
   PEANUT BUTTER SAUCE (recipe follows)

Heat oven to 325°F. Place pecans and butter in square baking pan; toast in oven about 7 minutes, stirring occasionally, until butter is melted and nuts are coated. Set aside to cool. Meanwhile, in medium microwave-safe bowl, place peanut butter chips and milk. Microwave at HIGH (100%) 1 minute; stir. If necessary, microwave an additional 15 seconds at a time, stirring after each heating, just until chips are melted when stirred; cool 10 minutes. In large mixer bowl, beat cream cheese and powdered sugar until fluffy; blend in peanut butter mixture. Prepare whipped topping mix according to package directions; fold in peanut butter mixture and 1/2 cup toasted pecans. Pour into crust. Wrap tightly; freeze several hours. Serve with warm PEANUT BUTTER SAUCE; garnish with remaining pecans. *6 to 8 servings.*

PEANUT BUTTER SAUCE

1   cup REESE'S Peanut Butter chips
1/3   cup milk
1/4   cup whipping cream
1/4   teaspoon vanilla extract

In medium microwave-safe bowl, place peanut butter chips, milk and whipping cream. Microwave at HIGH (100%) 2 to 2 1/2 minutes; stir. If necessary, microwave at HIGH an additional 30 seconds at a time, stirring after each heating, just until chips are melted when stirred. Stir in vanilla; serve warm. Refrigerate leftover sauce. *About 1 cup sauce.*

Chocolate Walnut Pie

6   tablespoons butter or margarine
1/3   cup HERSHEY'S Cocoa
1   can (14 oz.) sweetened condensed milk
1/2   cup water
2   eggs, beaten
1/2   teaspoon vanilla extract
1/2   teaspoon imitation maple flavor
1   cup coarsely chopped walnuts
   9-inch unbaked pastry shell

Heat oven to 350°F. In medium saucepan over low heat, melt butter. Add cocoa; stir until smooth. Stir in sweetened condensed milk, water and eggs; beat with wire whisk until well blended. Remove from heat; stir in vanilla, maple flavor and walnuts. Pour into pastry shell. Bake 40 to 45 minutes or until center is set. Cool slightly. Serve warm or cold. Garnish as desired. Refrigerate leftovers. *8 servings.*

Chocolate Rum Mousse Pie

The chocolate mousse layer and the topping can be made in just a few minutes; then refrigerate until serving.

    8- or 9-inch baked pastry shell
1 **teaspoon unflavored gelatin**
1 **tablespoon cold water**
2 **tablespoons boiling water**
1/2 **cup sugar**
1/3 **cup HERSHEY'S Premium European Style Cocoa**
1 **cup (1/2 pt.) cold whipping cream**
1 **teaspoon vanilla extract**
    RUM CREAM TOPPING (recipe follows)

Prepare pastry shell; cool. In small cup, sprinkle gelatin over cold water; let stand 1 minute to soften. Add boiling water; stir until gelatin is completely dissolved and mixture is clear. Cool slightly, about 5 minutes. Meanwhile, in small mixer bowl, stir together sugar and cocoa; add whipping cream and vanilla. Beat on medium speed of electric mixer, scraping bottom of bowl occasionally, until stiff; pour in gelatin mixture and beat just until well blended. Pour mixture into pastry shell. Spread RUM CREAM TOPPING over chocolate. Refrigerate at least 2 hours. *6 to 8 servings.*

RUM CREAM TOPPING: In small mixer bowl, beat 1 cup (1/2 pt.) cold whipping cream, 2 tablespoons powdered sugar and 2 teaspoons light rum or 1/2 teaspoon rum extract until stiff.

Chocolate Walnut Pie (top), recipe page 34;
Chocolate Rum Mousse Pie (bottom), recipe page 35.

Innkeeper Pie

This pie has a surprising light cake layer over a fudgey chocolate layer.

PASTRY CRUST (recipe follows)
2/3 **cup sugar**
1/3 **cup HERSHEY'S Cocoa**
1 **cup water**
1/3 **cup butter or margarine**
2 1/2 **teaspoons vanilla extract, divided**
1 **cup all-purpose flour**
3/4 **cup sugar**
1 **teaspoon baking powder**
1/2 **teaspoon salt**
1/4 **cup shortening**
1/2 **cup milk**
1 **egg**
1/2 **cup chopped nuts**
SWEETENED WHIPPED CREAM (recipe follows)

Heat oven to 350°F. Prepare PASTRY CRUST. In medium saucepan, stir together 2/3 cup sugar and cocoa; blend in water. Over medium heat, heat to boiling, stirring occasionally; boil and stir 1 minute. Remove from heat; add butter and 1 1/2 teaspoons vanilla, stirring until butter is melted. Set aside. In small mixer bowl, stir together flour, 3/4 cup sugar, baking powder and salt; add shortening, milk and remaining

1 teaspoon vanilla. Beat on medium speed of electric mixer 2 minutes. Add egg; beat 2 minutes. Spoon batter into prepared crust. Stir chocolate mixture; gently pour over batter. Sprinkle nuts over top. Bake 55 to 60 minutes or until wooden pick inserted in cake portion comes out clean. Cool slightly; serve warm with SWEETENED WHIPPED CREAM. *8 servings.*

PASTRY CRUST

1 1/3 **cups all-purpose flour**
1/2 **teaspoon salt**
1/8 **teaspoon baking powder**
1/2 **cup shortening**
3 **tablespoons cold water**

In medium bowl, stir together flour, salt and baking powder. Cut in shortening until particles are size of small peas; sprinkle in water, tossing with fork until all flour is moistened. Roll dough into circle about 1/8 inch thick. Fit into 9-inch pie plate; set aside.

SWEETENED WHIPPED CREAM: In small mixer bowl, combine 1 cup (1/2 pt.) cold whipping cream, 2 tablespoons sugar and 1 teaspoon vanilla extract; beat until stiff.

Chocolate Mousse and Praline Pie

This pie combines two classic desserts; the chocolate mousse layer is light and fluffy and the praline layer is similar to the traditional nut and caramel confection from the South.

- ¹/₃ **cup butter or margarine**
- ¹/₄ **cup packed light brown sugar**
- 2 **tablespoons water**
- 1 **tablespoon cornstarch**
- ²/₃ **cup coarsely chopped pecans**
  8-inch (6 oz.) packaged crumb crust
  CHOCOLATE MOUSSE FILLING (recipe follows)
  Pecan halves

In small microwave-safe bowl, place butter. Microwave at HIGH (100%) 1 minute or until melted. Add brown sugar, water and cornstarch; stir with wire whisk until smooth. Microwave at HIGH 1 minute or until mixture comes to full boil. Stir in chopped pecans; spread mixture on bottom of crust. Place crust in freezer while preparing filling. Prepare CHOCOLATE MOUSSE FILLING.

Carefully spread filling over pecan layer. Cover; refrigerate 3 to 4 hours. Garnish with pecan halves. Refrigerate leftovers. *6 to 8 servings.*

CHOCOLATE MOUSSE FILLING

- 1 **teaspoon unflavored gelatin**
- 1 **tablespoon cold water**
- 2 **tablespoons boiling water**
- ¹/₂ **cup sugar**
- ¹/₄ **cup HERSHEY'S Cocoa**
- 1 **cup (¹/₂ pt.) cold whipping cream**
- 1 **teaspoon vanilla extract**

In small cup, sprinkle gelatin over cold water; let stand 1 minute to soften. Add boiling water; stir until gelatin is completely dissolved and mixture is clear. Cool slightly, about 5 minutes. Meanwhile, in small mixer bowl, stir together sugar and cocoa; add whipping cream and vanilla. Beat on medium speed of electric mixer, scraping bottom of bowl occasionally, until stiff; pour in gelatin mixture and beat just until well blended.

Triple Decker Chocolate Coconut Cream Pie

Adding cocoa to the coconut cream filling creates a whole new taste combination.

> **9-inch baked pastry shell**
> 2/3 **cup sugar**
> 1/3 **cup cornstarch**
> 1/4 **teaspoon salt**
> 3 **cups milk**
> 3 **eggs, slightly beaten**
> 1 **tablespoon butter or margarine**
> 2 **teaspoons vanilla extract**
> 1/2 **cup flaked coconut**
> 3 **tablespoons HERSHEY'S Cocoa**
> 3 **tablespoons sugar**
> 2 **tablespoons milk**
> **Whipped topping**

Prepare pastry shell; cool. In medium saucepan, stir together 2/3 cup sugar, cornstarch, salt and 3 cups milk; blend in eggs. Cook over medium heat, stirring constantly, until mixture boils; boil and stir 1 minute. Remove from heat; stir in butter and vanilla. Into small bowl, pour 1 1/2 cups cream filling; stir in coconut. Set aside. In separate bowl, stir together cocoa, 3 tablespoons sugar and 2 tablespoons milk; blend into remaining cream filling in saucepan. Return to heat; heat just to boiling, stirring constantly. Remove from heat; pour 1 cup chocolate filling into pastry shell. Spread coconut filling over chocolate layer. Top with remaining chocolate filling; spread evenly. Cover with plastic wrap; refrigerate until cold. Just before serving, spread with whipped topping. *8 servings.*

Three-in-One Chocolate Pudding & Pie Filling

This recipe for a traditional rich creamy chocolate pudding is so versatile it can be used in pies, parfaits or simply as a pudding.

> 3/4 **cup sugar**
> 1/3 **cup HERSHEY'S Cocoa**
> 2 **tablespoons cornstarch**
> 2 **tablespoons all-purpose flour**
> 1/4 **teaspoon salt**
> 2 **cups milk**
> 2 **eggs, slightly beaten**
> 2 **tablespoons butter or margarine**
> 1 **teaspoon vanilla extract**

In medium saucepan, stir together sugar, cocoa, cornstarch, flour and salt; blend in milk and eggs. Cook over medium heat, stirring constantly, until mixture boils; boil and stir 1 minute. Remove from heat; stir in butter and vanilla. Pour into individual serving dishes; press plastic wrap directly onto surface. Cool; refrigerate. *4 servings.*

PARFAITS: Alternate layers of cold pudding and sweetened whipped cream or whipped topping in parfait glasses.

PIE: Reduce milk to 1 3/4 cups in recipe above; cook as directed. Stir in butter and vanilla. Pour hot pudding into 8-inch (6 oz.) packaged crumb crust; press plastic wrap onto surface. Refrigerate; top with sweetened whipped cream or whipped topping before serving. *6 servings.*

BAKER'S TIP

Cookie crumbs may be made by placing cookies in a heavy-duty plastic bag and crushing with a rolling pin until fine OR placing in a food processor and pulsing the blade until crumbs are fine.

Mocha Bavarian Pie

NUT CRUMB CRUST (recipe follows)
1 **envelope unflavored gelatin**
1²/₃ **cups milk, divided**
²/₃ **cup sugar**
¹/₃ **cup HERSHEY'S Cocoa**
³/₄ **teaspoon powdered instant coffee**
2 **tablespoons butter or margarine**
³/₄ **teaspoon vanilla extract**
¹/₂ **cup cold whipping cream**
COFFEE WHIPPED CREAM (recipe follows)

Prepare NUT CRUMB CRUST; cool. In medium saucepan, sprinkle gelatin over 1 cup milk; let stand 2 minutes. In small bowl, stir together sugar and cocoa; add to mixture in saucepan. Cook over medium heat, stirring constantly, until mixture boils; stir in instant coffee. Remove from heat; add butter, stirring until melted. Blend in remaining ²/₃ cup milk and vanilla; pour into large bowl. Cool; refrigerate until mixture just begins to set, stirring occasionally. In separate bowl, beat whipping cream until stiff peaks form; carefully fold into chocolate mixture, blending well. Pour into prepared crust; refrigerate until set. Garnish with COFFEE WHIPPED CREAM. *6 to 8 servings.*

NUT CRUMB CRUST

³/₄ **cup toasted ground pecans***
³/₄ **cup vanilla wafer crumbs (about 20 wafers)**
2 **tablespoons sugar**
3 **tablespoons butter or margarine, melted**

Heat oven to 350°F. In small bowl, combine pecans, crumbs and sugar; add butter, stirring until all crumbs are moistened. Press mixture evenly on bottom and up sides of 9-inch pie plate. Bake 8 minutes.

*To Toast Pecans: Heat oven to 350°F. Spread ³/₄ cup pecan pieces in thin layer in shallow baking pan. Bake 8 to 10 minutes, stirring occasionally; cool. Grind in food processor with metal blade.

COFFEE WHIPPED CREAM: In small mixer bowl, combine 1 cup (¹/₂ pt.) cold whipping cream, ¹/₄ cup powdered sugar, 1 tablespoon powdered instant coffee and ¹/₂ teaspoon vanilla extract; beat until stiff. *About 2 cups topping.*

39

CHEESECAKES

Creamy cheesecakes are so smooth and luscious they melt in your mouth while you savor all the tasty rewards. These irresistibly rich chocolate and peanut butter variations add a delightful new twist to traditional cheesecakes. Your family will soon consider these delicious desserts among their all-time favorites.

Chocolate Almond Cheesecake (top), recipe page 42; Paisley Print Cheesecake (bottom), recipe page 44.

Chocolate Almond Cheesecake

ALMOND CRUMB CRUST
(recipe follows)
3 packages (8 oz. each) cream cheese, softened
1 1/4 cups sugar
1/3 cup HERSHEY'S Cocoa
1/2 cup dairy sour cream
2 tablespoons all-purpose flour
2 teaspoons almond extract
1 teaspoon vanilla extract
3 eggs
ALMOND WHIPPED CREAM
(recipe follows)
Sliced almonds (optional)

Prepare ALMOND CRUMB CRUST; set aside. Heat oven to 425°F. In large mixer bowl, combine cream cheese, sugar, cocoa, sour cream and flour; beat on medium speed until smooth. Add almond and vanilla extracts and eggs; beat well. Pour into prepared crust. Bake 10 minutes. Reduce oven temperature to 250°F; continue baking 55 minutes or until center appears set. Remove from oven to cooling rack; loosen cake from rim of pan. Cool completely; remove rim. Cover; refrigerate. Garnish with ALMOND WHIPPED CREAM and sliced almonds, if desired. Cover; refrigerate leftovers. *10 to 12 servings.*

ALMOND CRUMB CRUST: Heat oven to 350°F. In small bowl, stir together 3/4 cup vanilla wafer crumbs (about 20 wafers), 1/2 cup ground blanched almonds and 3 tablespoons sugar; blend in 3 tablespoons melted butter or margarine, mixing well. Press mixture onto bottom and 1/2 inch up side of 9-inch springform pan. Bake 8 to 10 minutes; cool slightly.

ALMOND WHIPPED CREAM: In small mixer bowl, combine 1/2 cup cold whipping cream, 2 tablespoons powdered sugar, 1/4 teaspoon vanilla extract and 1/8 teaspoon almond extract; beat until stiff. *About 1 cup topping.*

Chocolate Chip Pumpkin Cheesecake

An ideal dessert to finish off your Thanksgiving dinner.

1 cup vanilla wafer crumbs (about 30 wafers)
1/4 cup HERSHEY'S Cocoa
1/4 cup powdered sugar
1/4 cup (1/2 stick) butter or margarine, melted
3 packages (8 oz. each) cream cheese, softened
1 cup granulated sugar
3 tablespoons all-purpose flour
1 teaspoon ground pumpkin pie spice
1 cup canned pumpkin
4 eggs
1 1/2 cups HERSHEY'S MINI CHIPS Semi-Sweet Chocolate
Chocolate leaves (optional)

Heat oven to 350°F. In medium bowl, combine crumbs, cocoa, and powdered sugar; stir in butter. Press mixture onto bottom and 1/2 inch up side of 9-inch springform pan. Bake 8 minutes; cool slightly. Increase oven temperature to 400°F. In large mixer bowl, beat cream cheese, granulated sugar, flour and pumpkin pie spice until well blended. Add pumpkin and eggs; beat until well blended. Stir in small chocolate chips; pour into prepared crust. Bake 10 minutes. Reduce oven temperature to 250°F; continue baking 50 minutes. Remove from oven to cooling rack; loosen cake from rim of pan. Cool completely; remove rim. Refrigerate. Garnish with chocolate leaves, if desired. Cover; refrigerate leftovers. *10 to 12 servings.*

Chocolate Drizzled Peanut Butter Cheesecake (left), recipe page 43; Chocolate Chip Pumpkin Cheesecake (right), recipe page 42.

Chocolate Drizzled Peanut Butter Cheesecake

This cheesecake combines those two great flavors, chocolate and peanut butter.

GRAHAM CRACKER CRUST
  (recipe follows)
- 3 **packages (8 oz. each) cream cheese, softened**
- 3/4 **cup sugar**
- 1 2/3 **cups (10-oz. package) REESE'S Peanut Butter Chips**
- 1/4 **cup milk**
- 4 **eggs**
- 1 **teaspoon vanilla extract**
  CHOCOLATE DRIZZLE
  (recipe follows)

Prepare GRAHAM CRACKER CRUST. Heat oven to 450°F. In large mixer bowl, combine cream cheese and sugar; beat on medium speed of electric mixer until smooth. In small microwave-safe bowl, place peanut butter chips with milk. Microwave at HIGH (100%) 1 minute; stir. If necessary, microwave at HIGH an additional 15 seconds at a time, stirring after each heating, just until chips are melted when stirred. Blend peanut butter chip mixture into cream cheese mixture. Add eggs, one at a time, mixing well after each addition. Stir in vanilla. Pour mixture over GRAHAM CRACKER CRUST. Bake 10 minutes. Reduce oven temperature to 250°F; continue baking 40 minutes. Remove from oven to cooling rack; loosen cake from rim of pan. Cool completely; remove rim. Prepare CHOCOLATE DRIZZLE; drizzle over cheesecake. Cover; refrigerate leftovers.
12 servings.

GRAHAM CRACKER CRUST: Heat oven to 325°F. In small bowl, stir together 1 cup graham cracker crumbs, 3 tablespoons sugar and 3 tablespoons melted butter or margarine. Press mixture onto bottom of 9-inch springform pan. Bake 10 minutes. Remove from oven.

CHOCOLATE DRIZZLE: In small microwave-safe bowl, place 1/2 cup HERSHEY'S Semi-Sweet Chocolate Chips and 1 tablespoon shortening. Microwave at HIGH (100%) 30 seconds; stir. If necessary, microwave at HIGH an additional 20 seconds or until chocolate is melted and mixture is smooth when stirred.

Paisley Print Cheesecake

GRAHAM CRUST (recipe follows)
- 3 packages (8 oz. each) cream cheese, softened
- 1 cup sugar, divided
- 1/2 cup dairy sour cream
- 2 1/2 teaspoons vanilla extract, divided
- 3 tablespoons all-purpose flour
- 3 eggs
- 1 1/2 squares (1 1/2 oz.) HERSHEY'S Unsweetened Baking Chocolate, broken into pieces

Prepare GRAHAM CRUST; set aside. Heat oven to 450°F. In large mixer bowl, combine cream cheese, 3/4 cup sugar, sour cream and 2 teaspoons vanilla; beat on medium speed of electric mixer until smooth. Add flour, 1 tablespoon at a time, blending well. Add eggs; beat well. In small microwave-safe bowl, place chocolate. Microwave at HIGH (100%) 1 to 1 1/2 minutes or just until chocolate is melted and smooth when stirred. Add 1 1/2 cups cream cheese mixture, remaining 1/4 cup sugar and remaining 1/2 teaspoon vanilla; blend well. Spoon plain and chocolate mixtures alternately into prepared crust, ending with dollops of chocolate on top; gently swirl with knife or spatula for paisley effect. Bake 10 minutes; decrease temperature to 250°F. Continue to bake 35 minutes. Remove from oven to cooling rack; loosen cake from rim of pan. Cool completely; remove rim. Cover; refrigerate leftovers. *10 to 12 servings.*

GRAHAM CRUST: Heat oven to 350°F. In small bowl, stir together 1 cup graham cracker crumbs and 2 tablespoons sugar; blend in 1/4 cup melted butter or margarine, mixing well. Press mixture onto bottom and 1/2 inch up side of 9-inch springform pan. Bake 8 to 10 minutes. Cool.

Chocolate Cheesecake

CHOCOLATE CRUMB CRUST (recipe follows)
- 1/4 cup butter or margarine
- 1/2 cup HERSHEY'S Cocoa
- 3 packages (8 oz. each) cream cheese, softened
- 1 can (14 oz.) sweetened condensed milk
- 4 eggs
- 1 tablespoon vanilla extract

Prepare CHOCOLATE CRUMB CRUST; set aside. Heat oven to 300°F. In medium microwave-safe bowl, place butter. Microwave at HIGH (100%) 30 to 45 seconds or until melted. Stir in cocoa until smooth; set aside. In large mixer bowl, beat cream cheese. Add cocoa mixture; beat well. Gradually beat in sweetened condensed milk until smooth. Add eggs and vanilla; beat well. Pour into prepared crust. Bake 1 hour and 5 minutes or until set. (Center will be soft.) Remove from oven to cooling rack; loosen cake from rim of pan. Cool completely; remove rim. Cover; refrigerate leftovers. *12 servings.*

CHOCOLATE CRUMB CRUST: In medium microwave-safe bowl, place 6 tablespoons butter or margarine. Microwave at HIGH (100%) 30 seconds or until melted. Stir in 1 1/2 cups vanilla wafer crumbs (about 45 wafers), 6 tablespoons powdered sugar and 6 tablespoons HERSHEY'S Cocoa; blend well. Press mixture onto bottom and 1/2 inch up side of 9-inch springform pan.

Raspberry Chocolate Swirl Cheesecake

CHOCOLATE CRUMB CRUST
(recipe follows)
3 packages (8 oz. each) cream cheese, softened
1 cup sugar, divided
1¹/2 teaspoons vanilla extract, divided
3 eggs
¹/4 cup HERSHEY'S Cocoa
1 tablespoon vegetable oil
²/3 cup seedless red raspberry preserves
3 tablespoons all-purpose flour
RASPBERRY SAUCE (recipe follows)
Raspberries (optional)

Prepare CHOCOLATE CRUMB CRUST; set aside. Heat oven to 425°F. In large mixer bowl, beat cream cheese, ³/4 cup sugar and 1 teaspoon vanilla until smooth. Add eggs; beat until well blended. In small bowl, stir together cocoa and remaining ¹/4 cup sugar. Add oil, remaining ¹/2 teaspoon vanilla and 1¹/2 cups cheese mixture; blend well. Stir preserves to soften. Add preserves and flour to remaining cheese mixture in bowl; blend well. Pour half of raspberry mixture into pan; dollop about half of chocolate mixture onto raspberry.

Repeat with remaining mixture ending with chocolate dollops on top; gently swirl with knife or metal spatula for marbled effect. Bake 10 minutes. Reduce oven temperature to 250°F; continue baking 55 minutes or until center appears set. Remove pan from oven to wire rack; loosen cake from rim of pan. Cool completely; remove rim. Cover; refrigerate leftovers. Serve with RASPBERRY SAUCE and raspberries, if desired. *10 to 12 servings.*

CHOCOLATE CRUMB CRUST: Heat oven to 350°F. In medium bowl, combine 1¹/4 cups vanilla wafer crumbs (about 40 wafers), ¹/4 cup HERSHEY'S Cocoa and ¹/4 cup powdered sugar. Stir in ¹/4 cup melted butter or margarine. Press mixture onto bottom and ¹/2 inch up side of 9-inch springform pan. Bake 8 to 10 minutes; cool slightly.

RASPBERRY SAUCE: In small saucepan, stir together ¹/4 cup sugar and 2 teaspoons cornstarch; stir in 1 package (10 oz.) frozen red raspberries in light syrup, thawed. Heat to boiling, stirring constantly; boil and stir 1 minute. Cool; press through sieve to remove seeds. *About 1 cup sauce.*

Neapolitan Cheesecake ▼

CHOCOLATE CRUMB CRUST
(recipe follows)
1 **package (10 oz.) frozen strawberries, thawed and drained thoroughly**
1/2 **cup HERSHEY'S Semi-Sweet Chocolate Chips**
3 **packages (8 oz. each) cream cheese, softened**
1 1/2 **cups sugar**
3 **eggs**
1/3 **cup dairy sour cream**
3 **tablespoons plus 1 teaspoon all-purpose flour, divided**
1/2 **teaspoon vanilla extract**
1/4 **teaspoon salt**
1/4 **teaspoon red food color (optional)**

Prepare CHOCOLATE CRUMB CRUST. Heat oven to 400°F. In blender or food processor, purée strawberries to yield 1/2 cup; set aside. In small microwave-safe bowl, place chocolate chips. Microwave at HIGH (100%) 1 1/2 minutes; stir. If necessary, microwave at HIGH an additional 15 seconds at a time, stirring after each heating, just until chips are melted when stirred; set aside. In large mixer bowl, beat cream cheese with sugar until smooth. Blend in eggs, sour cream, flour, vanilla and salt; beat until smooth. In separate bowl, stir together 1 1/3 cups batter and remaining 1 teaspoon flour with strawberries; add food color, if desired. Pour strawberry batter into crust. Carefully spoon 2 cups vanilla batter over strawberry batter; smooth surface. Stir melted chocolate into remaining batter; carefully spoon over vanilla batter, smoothing surface. Bake 10 minutes. Reduce oven temperature to 350°F; continue baking 55 to 60 minutes or until center is almost set. Remove from oven to cooling rack. Cool 30 minutes. Loosen cake from rim of pan; cool to room temperature. Refrigerate several hours or overnight; remove rim of pan. Cover; refrigerate leftovers. *10 to 12 servings.*

CHOCOLATE CRUMB CRUST: Heat oven to 350°F. In small bowl, stir together 1 1/2 cups vanilla wafer crumbs (about 45 wafers), 1/2 cup powdered sugar and 1/4 cup HERSHEY'S Cocoa; blend in 1/3 cup melted butter or margarine. Press mixture onto bottom of 9-inch springform pan. Bake 8 minutes.

Chocolate Ribbon Cheesecake ▼

WALNUT CRUMB CRUST
(recipe follows)
1/4 **cup (1/2 stick) butter or**
margarine, melted
1/3 **cup HERSHEY'S Cocoa**
3 **packages (8 oz. each) cream**
cheese, softened
1 **can (14 oz.) sweetened**
condensed milk
3 **eggs**
1 **tablespoon vanilla extract**

Prepare WALNUT CRUMB CRUST; set aside. Heat oven to 300°F. In small bowl, stir together butter and cocoa until smooth; set aside. In large mixer bowl, beat cream cheese until fluffy. Gradually beat in sweetened condensed milk until smooth. Beat in eggs and vanilla. Remove 1 1/2 cups batter; set aside.

Add cocoa mixture to remaining batter in mixer bowl; beat well. Pour half of chocolate batter into crust; top with half of vanilla batter. Repeat, ending with vanilla batter; gently swirl with metal spatula or knife for marbled effect. Bake 1 hour and 5 minutes or until center is set. Remove from oven to cooling rack. Cool 30 minutes. Loosen cake from rim of pan; cool to room temperature. Refrigerate several hours; remove rim. Cover; refrigerate leftovers. *10 to 12 servings.*

WALNUT CRUMB CRUST: In bowl, stir together 1 cup finely chopped walnuts, 1 cup graham cracker crumbs, 1/4 cup sugar and 1/4 cup (1/2 stick) melted butter or margarine. Press mixture firmly onto bottom and 2 inches up side of 9-inch springform pan.

Easy No-Bake Peanut Butter Cheesecake

Smooth and soft, this peanutty rich cheesecake is perfect for those times when you don't want to bake.

    CHOCOLATE CRUMB CRUST (recipe follows)
1 **package (8 oz.) cream cheese, softened**
2 **tablespoons lemon juice**
1²/₃ **cups (10-oz. package) REESE'S Peanut Butter Chips**
1 **can (14 oz.) sweetened condensed milk**
1 **cup (¹/₂ pt.) cold whipping cream**
    Sliced fresh fruit (optional)

Prepare CHOCOLATE CRUMB CRUST; set aside. In large mixer bowl, beat cream cheese with lemon juice until fluffy. In medium saucepan, combine peanut butter chips and sweetened condensed milk; stir constantly over low heat until chips are melted and mixture is smooth. Add to cream cheese mixture; blend well. In small mixer bowl, beat whipping cream until stiff. Fold into cream cheese mixture. Pour over crust. Cover; refrigerate until firm. Garnish as desired. *12 servings.*

CHOCOLATE CRUMB CRUST

1¹/₄ **cups graham cracker crumbs**
¹/₄ **cup HERSHEY'S Cocoa**
¹/₄ **cup powdered sugar**
¹/₄ **cup (¹/₂ stick) butter or margarine, melted**

In small bowl, stir together crumbs, cocoa, powdered sugar and butter. Press firmly onto bottom of 9-inch springform pan.

48

Black Forest Mini Cheesecakes

Perfect for any get-together, these mini cheesecakes are named for the famous Black Forest region of Germany.

18	to 24 vanilla wafer cookies
2	packages (8 oz. each) cream cheese, softened
1 1/4	cups sugar
1/3	cup HERSHEY'S Cocoa
2	tablespoons all-purpose flour
3	eggs
1	cup (8 oz.) dairy sour cream
1/2	teaspoon almond extract
	SOUR CREAM TOPPING (recipe follows)
	Canned cherry pie filling, chilled

Heat oven to 325°F. Line muffin pans (2 1/2 inches in diameter) with foil laminated baking cups. Place one vanilla wafer on bottom of each cup.

In large mixer bowl, beat cream cheese until smooth. Add sugar, cocoa and flour; blend well. Add eggs; beat well. Stir in sour cream and almond extract. Fill each prepared cup almost full with cheese mixture. Bake 20 to 25 minutes or until set. Remove from oven; cool 5 to 10 minutes. Spread heaping teaspoonful SOUR CREAM TOPPING on each cup. Cool completely in pans; refrigerate. Garnish with dollop of cherry pie filling just before serving. Refrigerate leftovers. *1 1/2 to 2 dozen cheesecakes.*

SOUR CREAM TOPPING: In small bowl, stir together 1 cup (8 oz.) dairy sour cream, 2 tablespoons sugar and 1 teaspoon vanilla extract; stir until sugar is dissolved.

CANDIES & SNACKS

Treat yourself, your family and your guests to delicious chocolate sweets! There's no need to take a trip to the candy store when you can create these tempting treats in your own kitchen. Indulge your chocolate lover's sweet tooth with several of these bite-size goodies made even more special when you make them yourself, from scratch!

Clockwise from Left: Double Peanut Truffles, recipe page 52; Chocolate Nut Clusters, recipe page 57; Rich Cocoa Fudge, recipe page 52.

Double Peanut Truffles

A trick to making truffles is to keep your room cool and to periodically dip your hands in ice water to keep them cold (be sure to dry them before rolling the mixture into balls).

1²/3 cups (10-oz. package)
    REESE'S Peanut Butter Chips
  1 cup (¹/2 pt.) whipping cream
 ¹/4 cup finely chopped peanuts
 ¹/2 cup powdered sugar
 ¹/4 cup HERSHEY'S Premium
    European Style Cocoa

Butter 8- or 9-inch square pan; set aside. In medium saucepan, stir together peanut butter chips, whipping cream and peanuts. Cook over low heat, stirring constantly, until chips are melted and mixture is well blended. Pour mixture into prepared pan; refrigerate 2 hours or until firm. In small bowl, stir together powdered sugar and cocoa. To prepare truffles, with hands, roll small spoonfuls of mixture into ³/4-inch balls. Gently roll balls in cocoa mixture, coating all sides. Store in refrigerator. Reroll truffles in cocoa mixture before serving, if desired. *About 5 dozen truffles.*

BAKER'S TIP

Candy making will be most successful if the weather is cool and dry. Use an accurate candy thermometer and follow directions closely. Test your thermometer by placing it in a pan of boiling water. An accurate thermometer will register 212°F at sea level. Add or subtract degrees from cooking temperatures in recipes according to the thermometer reading. If you live at higher altitudes, check with a county extension agent to determine when water should boil in your area. Do not allow bottom of thermometer to touch bottom of pan.

Rich Cocoa Fudge

This is the recipe your grandmother used to make and one of our most requested recipes.

3 cups sugar
²/3 cup HERSHEY'S Cocoa or
    HERSHEY'S Premium
    European Style Cocoa
¹/8 teaspoon salt
1¹/2 cups milk
¹/4 cup (¹/2 stick) butter or
    margarine
1 teaspoon vanilla extract

Line 8- or 9-inch square pan with foil; butter foil. Set aside. In heavy 4-quart saucepan, stir together sugar, cocoa and salt; stir in milk. Cook over medium heat, stirring constantly, until mixture comes to full rolling boil. Boil, without stirring, to 234°F or until syrup, when dropped into very cold water, forms a soft ball which flattens when removed from water. (Bulb of candy thermometer should not rest on bottom of saucepan.) Remove from heat. Add butter and vanilla. DO NOT STIR. Cool at room temperature to 110°F (lukewarm). Beat with wooden spoon until fudge thickens and loses some of its gloss. Quickly spread into prepared pan; cool. Cut into squares. *About 36 pieces or 1³/4 pounds.*

VARIATIONS:

NUTTY RICH COCOA FUDGE: Beat cooked fudge as directed. Immediately stir in 1 cup broken almonds, pecans or walnuts and quickly spread into prepared pan.

MARSHMALLOW-NUT COCOA FUDGE: Increase cocoa to ³/4 cup. Cook fudge as directed. Add 1 cup marshmallow creme with butter and vanilla. DO NOT STIR. Cool to 110°F (lukewarm). Beat 10 minutes; stir in 1 cup broken nuts and pour into prepared pan. (Fudge does not set until poured into pan.)

Chocolate-Covered Almond Apricot Tassies

The name "tassies" comes from the miniature muffin pans used to shape the rich cocoa and fruit mixture. These tassies are perfect for gift giving.

2 cups vanilla wafer crumbs (about 60 wafers)
1 cup finely chopped almonds
1/3 cup HERSHEY'S Cocoa
1 can (14 oz.) sweetened condensed milk
1 package (8 oz.) dried apricots, chopped
1/2 cup chopped candied cherries
1/4 teaspoon almond extract
2 cups (11.5-oz. package) HERSHEY'S Milk Chocolate Chips
4 teaspoons shortening

Line miniature muffin cups with paper liners. In large bowl, combine crumbs, almonds and cocoa. Add sweetened condensed milk, apricots, cherries and almond extract; mix well. Refrigerate 30 minutes. Roll mixture into 1-inch balls; press into prepared muffin cups. In medium microwave-safe bowl, place chocolate chips and shortening. Microwave at HIGH (100%) 1 1/2 minutes; stir. If necessary, microwave at HIGH an additional 15 seconds at a time, stirring after each heating, just until chips are melted when stirred. Spoon 1 teaspoonful melted chocolate over each filled cup. Refrigerate until chocolate is set. Store, covered, in refrigerator. *About 6 dozen pieces candy.*

Chocolate-Almond Fudge

Many people have known this candy as Million Dollar Fudge.

4 cups sugar
1 jar (7 oz.) marshmallow creme
1 1/2 cups (12-oz. can) evaporated milk
1 tablespoon butter or margarine
2 cups (12-oz. package) HERSHEY'S Semi-Sweet Chocolate Chips
1 HERSHEY'S Milk Chocolate Bar (7 oz.), broken into pieces
1 teaspoon vanilla extract
3/4 cup slivered almonds, toasted and coarsely chopped*

Line 9-inch square pan with foil; set aside. In heavy 4-quart saucepan, stir together sugar, marshmallow creme, evaporated milk and butter. Cook over medium heat, stirring constantly, until mixture comes to full rolling boil; boil, stirring constantly, 7 minutes. Remove from heat; immediately add chocolate chips and chocolate bar pieces, stirring until chocolate is melted and mixture is smooth. Stir in vanilla and almonds. Pour into prepared pan; cool until firm. Cut into 1-inch squares. Store in tightly covered container. *About 5 dozen squares or about 4 pounds.*

*To toast almonds: Heat oven to 350°F. Spread almonds in thin layer in shallow baking pan. Bake 8 to 10 minutes, stirring occasionally, until light golden brown; cool.

BAKER'S TIP

Homemade candies make great gifts for the holidays or just as a thank-you for something special. Colorful candy or nut cups may be purchased at candy supply or speciality food stores and add a festive appearance to your efforts. Try mixing several different candy recipes in a decorative tin or box. Include a hand-written copy of the recipe, and you'll have a gift that no one will want to return.

Peanutty Rocky Road

2 cups (12-oz. package)
   HERSHEY'S MINI CHIPS
   Semi-Sweet Chocolate
1 cup HERSHEY'S Milk
   Chocolate Chips
1 can (14 oz.) sweetened
   condensed milk
1 1/2 teaspoons vanilla extract
   Dash salt
1 2/3 cups (10-oz. package) REESE'S
   Peanut Butter Chips
1 1/2 cups miniature marshmallows

Line 8-inch square pan with foil; set
aside. In large microwave-safe bowl,
place small chocolate chips and milk
chocolate chips. Microwave at HIGH
(100%) 1 1/2 minutes; stir. Microwave
at HIGH an additional 30 seconds at a
time, stirring after each heating, just
until chips are melted when stirred.
Stir in sweetened condensed milk,
vanilla and salt; blend well. Fold in
peanut butter chips and marshmallows. Immediately spread mixture
evenly in prepared pan. Refrigerate
2 hours or until firm. Invert onto
cutting board. Remove foil; cut into
squares. *About 5 dozen pieces.*

*Top to Bottom: Chocolate-Almond Fudge, recipe
page 53; Peanutty Rocky Road, recipe page 55;
Chocolate-Covered Almond Apricot Tassies, recipe
page 53; Chocolatey Peanut Brittle, recipe page 55.*

Chocolatey Peanut Brittle

*Adding chocolate to peanut brittle
makes this brittle taste different from
any you've ever had before.*

1/4 cup HERSHEY'S Cocoa
1 teaspoon baking soda
1 tablespoon butter
1 cup sugar
1/2 cup light corn syrup
1/4 cup whipping cream
1 1/4 cups salted peanuts

Lightly butter a cookie sheet; set aside.
In small bowl, stir together cocoa and
baking soda; add butter. Set aside. In
heavy 2-quart saucepan, stir together
sugar, corn syrup and whipping cream.
Cook over medium heat, stirring constantly until sugar is dissolved. Stir in
peanuts. Continue cooking, stirring
frequently, until mixture reaches
300°F on candy thermometer OR
when syrup dropped into very cold
water separates into threads which
are hard and brittle. (Bulb of candy
thermometer should not rest on bottom of saucepan.) Remove from heat;
stir in cocoa mixture. Immediately
pour onto prepared cookie sheet.
With tongs or wooden spoons, quickly spread and pull into 1/4-inch thick-
ness. Place cookie sheet on wire rack;
cool completely. Snap into pieces;
store in tightly covered container.
About 1 pound candy.

BAKER'S TIP

DO NOT allow chocolate to come in contact with moisture during melting
since this can cause lumping, tightening or "seizing." If this occurs, add one
to two tablespoons shortening for every six ounces chocolate (do not use
butter or margarine since these may contain water); stir until fluid.

Creamy Double Decker Fudge

1 cup REESE'S Peanut Butter Chips
1 can (14 oz.) sweetened
   condensed milk, divided
1 teaspoon vanilla extract, divided
1 cup HERSHEY'S Semi-Sweet
   Chocolate Chips

Line 8-inch square pan with foil; set aside. In small microwave-safe bowl, place peanut butter chips and 2/3 cup sweetened condensed milk. Microwave at HIGH (100%) 1 to 1 1/2 minutes, stirring after 1 minute, until chips are melted and mixture is smooth when stirred. Stir in 1/2 teaspoon vanilla; spread evenly into prepared pan. In small microwave-safe bowl, place remaining sweetened condensed milk and chocolate chips; repeat above microwave procedure. Stir in remaining 1/2 teaspoon vanilla; spread evenly over peanut butter layer. Cover; refrigerate until firm. Cut into 1-inch squares. Store in tightly covered container in refrigerator. *About 4 dozen squares or 1 1/2 pounds.*

Semi-Sweet Chocolate Fudge

4 cups sugar
1 jar (7 oz.) marshmallow creme
1 1/2 cups (12-oz. can) evaporated
   milk
1 tablespoon butter or
   margarine
4 cups (24-oz. package)
   HERSHEY'S Semi-Sweet
   Chocolate Chips

Line 13 × 9 × 2-inch pan with foil, extending foil over edges of pan. Butter foil lightly; set aside. In heavy 4-quart saucepan, stir together sugar, marshmallow creme, evaporated milk and butter. Cook over medium heat, stirring constantly, until mixture comes to full rolling boil; boil and stir 5 minutes. Remove from heat; immediately add chocolate chips, stirring until smooth. Pour into prepared pan; cool until firm. Use foil to lift fudge out of pan; peel off foil. Cut into squares. Store tightly covered in a cool, dry place. *About 8 dozen squares.*

Cocoa Nut Break-Up

3/4 **cup butter**
1 **cup sugar**
1/4 **cup HERSHEY'S Cocoa**
2 **tablespoons corn syrup**
2 **tablespoons water**
3/4 **cup coarsely chopped pecans
    or toasted slivered almonds**

Melt butter in saucepan; stir in sugar, cocoa, corn syrup and water. Cook over medium heat, stirring constantly to 260°F on candy thermometer OR until syrup, when dropped into very cold water, separates into threads which are hard but not brittle. (Bulb of candy thermometer should not rest on bottom of saucepan.) Remove from heat; stir in nuts. Immediately spread mixture about 1/4 inch thick onto ungreased cookie sheet. Cool on wire rack. Refrigerate until cold. Remove from sheet; break into serving-size pieces. Store in tightly covered container in refrigerator. *About 1 1/2 pounds.*

Left to Right: Creamy Double Decker Fudge, Semi-Sweet Chocolate Fudge, recipes page 56; Cocoa Nut Break-Up, recipe page 57.

Chocolate Nut Clusters

These easy-to-make chocolate treats make great gifts.

1 **cup HERSHEY'S Milk Chocolate
    Chips**
1 **teaspoon shortening**
1 **cup broken pecans or walnuts**

In medium microwave-safe bowl, place chips and shortening. Microwave at HIGH (100%) 1 to 1 1/2 minutes or until smooth when stirred. Stir in nuts. Spoon heaping teaspoonfuls mixture into 1-inch paper candy cups or paper-lined mini muffin cups, filling each cup half full. Refrigerate until firm. Peel off paper cup, if desired. *14 to 16 candies.*

Vanilla-Covered
Strawberries ▲

1²/₃ cups (10-oz. package)
     HERSHEY'S Vanilla Milk Chips
1 tablespoon butter-flavored
     shortening
     Fresh strawberries, rinsed
     and patted dry

In medium microwave-safe bowl, place
vanilla milk chips and shortening. Microwave at HIGH (100%) 30 seconds; stir.
Microwave additional 15 seconds at a
time until smooth. Holding by top, dip
²/₃ of each strawberry into vanilla mixture; shake gently to remove excess.
Place on wax paper-covered tray.
Refrigerate until coating is firm. Store,
covered, in refrigerator. *About ³/₄
cup coating.*

Chocolate Snack Blocks ▲

*If your kids like the fruit gelatin snacks,
they'll love these chocolate snacks!*

3 envelopes unflavored gelatin
³/₄ cup cold water
1 cup boiling water
¹/₃ cup sugar
2 cups (12-oz. package)
     HERSHEY'S MINI CHIPS
     Semi-Sweet Chocolate

In blender, sprinkle gelatin over cold
water; let stand 5 minutes. Add boiling
water and sugar; cover, blending on
low speed until gelatin is completely
dissolved, about 2 minutes. Continue
to blend, gradually adding small chocolate chips, until chips are melted and
mixture is smooth. Pour into 8- or
9-inch square pan. Refrigerate until
firm. Cut into 1-inch squares or shapes
with cookie cutters. *About 6 dozen
squares.*

Vanilla Chip Trail Mix ▲

A perfect after-school snack.

- 1/2 **cup (1 stick) margarine, melted**
- 2 **tablespoons HERSHEY'S Cocoa**
- 2 **tablespoons sugar**
- 4 **cups toasted oat cereal rings**
- 4 **cups bite-size crisp wheat squares cereal**
- 1 **cup slivered almonds**
- 1 **cup golden raisins**
- 1 2/3 **cups (10-oz. package) HERSHEY'S Vanilla Milk Chips**

Heat oven to 250°F. In small bowl, stir together melted margarine, cocoa and sugar. In large bowl, combine cereals and almonds; stir in margarine mixture. Toss until ingredients are well coated. Pour mixture into 13 × 9 × 2-inch baking pan. Bake 1 hour, stirring every 15 minutes. Cool completely; stir in raisins and vanilla milk chips. Store in tightly covered container in cool, dry place. *About 11 1/2 cups snack mix.*

MICROWAVE INSTRUCTIONS:

In 4-quart microwave-safe bowl, place margarine. Microwave at HIGH (100%) 1 minute or until melted; stir in cocoa and sugar. Add cereals and almonds; stir until evenly coated. Microwave at HIGH 3 minutes, stirring every minute; stir in raisins. Microwave at HIGH additional 3 minutes, stirring every minute. Cool completely; stir in vanilla milk chips. Store in tightly covered container in cool, dry place.

COOKIES

Remember the excitement of grabbing a delicious homemade cookie from Grandma's cookie jar — and not being caught? Capture those joyful memories and share them with your own family when you bake these scrumptious, hand-held goodies from scratch. Pair fresh-baked cookies with a cool glass of milk for a delicious, old-fashioned snack that's still a favorite today.

REESE'S Chewy Chocolate Cookies (left), recipe page 66; HERSHEY'S Great American Chocolate Chip Cookies (right), recipe page 64.

Almond Orange Dainties ▲

These delicate orange-flavored cookies are topped with a rich chocolate filling.

1 1/2 cups (3 sticks) butter or
        margarine, softened
  3/4   cup sugar
1 1/2   teaspoons vanilla extract
    3   egg yolks
    3   cups all-purpose flour
  3/4   teaspoon baking powder
  1/2   teaspoon salt
    2   to 3 teaspoons freshly grated
        orange peel
        CHOCOLATE FILLING (recipe
        follows)
    1   cup toasted sliced almonds,
        ground*

In large mixer bowl, beat butter, sugar, vanilla and egg yolks until creamy. In separate bowl, stir together flour, baking powder and salt; gradually add to butter mixture, blending well. Stir in orange peel. Cover; refrigerate about 1 hour or until firm enough to handle. Meanwhile, prepare CHOCOLATE FILLING. Heat oven to 325°F. Shape dough into 1-inch balls; roll in ground almonds. Place about 2 inches apart on ungreased cookie sheet. Press thumb in center of each ball; spoon about 1/4 teaspoon filling in each thumbprint. Bake 11 to 13 minutes or until set. Cool slightly; remove

from cookie sheet to wire rack. Cool completely. *About 5 dozen cookies.*

CHOCOLATE FILLING

  1/3   cup sugar
  1/4   cup HERSHEY'S Cocoa
    1   tablespoon all-purpose flour
  1/2   cup whipping cream
    1   egg yolk, slightly beaten
    2   tablespoons butter or
        margarine
  1/2   teaspoon vanilla extract

In small saucepan, stir together sugar, cocoa and flour. Gradually stir in whipping cream. Cook over low heat, stirring constantly, until mixture comes to a boil. Blend small amount hot mixture into egg yolk. Return to saucepan; blend well. Cook over low heat, stirring constantly, 1 minute. Remove from heat. Add butter and vanilla; stir until mixture is smooth. Refrigerate until ready to use.

*To toast almonds: Heat oven to 350°F. Spread almonds in thin layer in shallow baking pan. Bake 8 to 10 minutes, stirring occasionally, until light golden brown; cool.

Chocolate Almond Biscotti ▲

Biscotti means twice baked. These unusual cookies are not difficult to make and are perfect for dunking in coffee.

1/2 cup (1 stick) butter or
    margarine, softened
1 1/4 cups sugar
2 eggs
1 teaspoon almond extract
2 1/4 cups all-purpose flour
1/4 cup HERSHEY'S Premium
    European Style Cocoa or
    HERSHEY'S Cocoa
1 teaspoon baking powder
1/4 teaspoon salt
1 cup sliced almonds
    CHOCOLATE GLAZE (recipe
    follows)
    VANILLA GLAZE (recipe
    follows)
    Additional sliced almonds
    (optional)

Heat oven to 350°F. In large mixer bowl, beat butter and sugar until well blended. Add eggs and almond extract; beat until smooth. In separate bowl, stir together flour, cocoa, baking powder and salt; blend into butter mixture, beating until smooth. (Dough will be thick.) Using wooden spoon, work almonds into dough. Divide dough into halves. With lightly floured hands, shape each half into rectangular log·about 2 inches in di-ameter and 11 inches long; place on large ungreased cookie sheet, at least 2 inches apart. Bake 30 minutes or until logs are set. Remove from oven; cool on cookie sheet 15 minutes. Using serrated knife and a sawing motion, cut logs into 1/2-inch diagonal slices. Discard end pieces. Arrange slices, cut sides down, close together on cookie sheet. Bake 8 to 9 minutes. Turn each slice over; bake additional 8 to 9 minutes. Remove from oven; cool on cookie sheet on wire rack. Drizzle CHOCOLATE GLAZE over each biscotti or dip end of each cookie into glaze. Drizzle VANILLA GLAZE over chocolate glaze. Garnish with additional almonds, if desired. *About 2 1/2 dozen cookies.*

CHOCOLATE GLAZE: In small microwave-safe bowl, place 1 cup HERSHEY'S Semi-Sweet Chocolate Chips and 1 tablespoon shortening. Microwave at HIGH (100%) 1 to 1 1/2 minutes or until smooth when stirred. *About 1 cup glaze.*

VANILLA GLAZE: In small microwave-safe bowl, place 1/4 cup HERSHEY'S Vanilla Milk Chips and 1 teaspoon shortening. Microwave at HIGH (100%) 30 to 45 seconds or until smooth when stirred. *About 1/4 cup glaze.*

HERSHEY'S Great American Chocolate Chip Cookies

This is our famous recipe for traditional chocolate chip cookies.

- 1 cup (2 sticks) butter, softened
- 3/4 cup granulated sugar
- 3/4 cup packed light brown sugar
- 1 teaspoon vanilla extract
- 2 eggs
- 2 1/4 cups all-purpose flour
- 1 teaspoon baking soda
- 1/2 teaspoon salt
- 2 cups (12-oz. package) HERSHEY'S Semi-Sweet Chocolate Chips
- 1 cup chopped nuts (optional)

Heat oven to 375°F. In large mixer bowl, beat butter, sugars and vanilla until light and fluffy. Add eggs; beat well. In separate bowl, stir together flour, baking soda and salt; gradually add to butter mixture. Beat well. Stir in chocolate chips and nuts, if desired. Drop by rounded teaspoonfuls onto ungreased cookie sheet. Bake 8 to 10 minutes or until lightly browned. Cool slightly; remove from cookie sheet to wire rack. Cool completely. *About 6 dozen cookies.*

PAN RECIPE: Spread in greased 15 1/2 × 10 1/2 × 1-inch jelly roll pan. Bake at 375°F, 20 minutes or until lightly browned. Cool completely; cut into bars. *About 4 dozen bars.*

SKOR & CHOCOLATE CHIP COOKIES: Use 1 cup finely chopped SKOR bars and 1 cup HERSHEY'S Semi-Sweet Chocolate Chips in place of 2 cups chocolate chips; omit nuts. Drop and bake as directed.

ICE CREAM SANDWICH: Press one small scoop of vanilla ice cream between two cookies.

Chocolate Clouds ▲

Light and airy, Chocolate Clouds are meringue puffs filled with chocolate.

- 3 egg whites
- 1/8 teaspoon cream of tartar
- 3/4 cup sugar
- 1 teaspoon vanilla extract
- 2 tablespoons HERSHEY'S Cocoa
- 1 3/4 cups (10-oz. package) HERSHEY'S Premium Semi-Sweet Chocolate Chunks OR 2 cups (12-oz.package) HERSHEY'S Semi-Sweet Chocolate Chips

Heat oven to 300°F. Place parchment paper or foil on cookie sheet. In large mixer bowl, beat egg whites and cream of tartar until soft peaks form. Gradually add sugar and vanilla, beating until stiff peaks hold, sugar is dissolved and mixture is glossy. Sift cocoa onto egg white mixture; gently fold just until combined. Fold in chocolate chunks. Drop by heaping tablespoonfuls onto prepared cookie sheet. Bake 35 to 45 minutes or just until dry. Carefully peel cookies off paper; cool completely on wire rack. Store, covered, at room temperature. *About 2 1/2 dozen cookies.*

Oatmeal Brownie Drops ▲

3/4 cup sugar
1/2 cup (1 stick) butter or
    margarine, softened
  2 eggs
  1 teaspoon vanilla extract
  1 cup all-purpose flour
1/2 cup HERSHEY'S Cocoa
1/4 teaspoon baking soda
  1 cup quick-cooking rolled oats
  1 cup HERSHEY'S MINI CHIPS
    Semi-Sweet Chocolate

Heat oven to 350°F. In large mixer bowl, beat together sugar and butter until well blended. Add eggs and vanilla, blend thoroughly. In small bowl, stir together flour, cocoa and baking soda; add to butter mixture, blending thoroughly. Stir in oatmeal and MINI 'CHIPS. Drop by tablespoons onto ungreased cookie sheet. Bake 7 to 8 minutes or until cookies begin to set. Do not overbake. Remove from cookie sheet to wire rack. Cool completely. *About 3 1/2 dozen cookies.*

Cocoa KISS Cookies ▲

Hidden inside each cookie is a HERSHEY'S KISS!

  1 cup (2 sticks) butter or
    margarine, softened
2/3 cup sugar
  1 teaspoon vanilla extract
1 2/3 cups all-purpose flour
1/4 cup HERSHEY'S Cocoa
  1 cup finely chopped pecans
  1 bag (9 oz.) HERSHEY'S KISSES
    Chocolates, unwrapped
    Powdered sugar

In large mixer bowl, beat butter, sugar and vanilla until creamy. In separate bowl, stir together flour and cocoa; blend into butter mixture. Add pecans; beat on low speed until well blended. Refrigerate dough about 1 hour or until firm enough to handle. Heat oven to 375°F. Mold scant tablespoon of dough around each unwrapped chocolate piece, covering chocolate piece completely. Shape into balls; place on ungreased cookie sheet. Bake 10 to 12 minutes or until set. Cool slightly; remove from cookie sheet to wire rack. Cool completely. Roll in powdered sugar. Roll in sugar again before serving, if desired. *About 4 1/2 dozen cookies.*

65

REESE'S Chewy Chocolate Cookies

1 1/4 cups (2 1/2 sticks) butter or margarine, softened
2 cups sugar
2 eggs
2 teaspoons vanilla extract
2 cups all-purpose flour
3/4 cup HERSHEY'S Cocoa
1 teaspoon baking soda
1/2 teaspoon salt
1 2/3 cups (10-oz. package) REESE'S Peanut Butter Chips

Heat oven to 350°F. In large mixer bowl, beat butter and sugar until light and fluffy. Add eggs and vanilla; beat well. Stir together flour, cocoa, baking soda and salt; gradually blend into butter mixture. Stir in chips. Drop by rounded teaspoonfuls onto ungreased cookie sheet. Bake 8 to 9 minutes. (Do not overbake; cookies will be soft. They will puff while baking and flatten while cooling). Cool slightly; remove from cookie sheet to wire rack. Cool completely. *About 4 1/2 dozen cookies.*

Cocoa Oatmeal Treats

These easy, no-bake candy-cookies have been a favorite for generations.

2 cups sugar
1/3 cup HERSHEY'S Cocoa
1/2 cup milk
1/2 cup (1 stick) butter or margarine
1/3 cup creamy peanut butter
2 1/2 cups quick-cooking rolled oats
1/2 cup chopped unsalted peanuts

In medium saucepan, stir together sugar and cocoa; stir in milk and butter. Cook over medium heat, stirring constantly, until mixture comes to a boil; boil 1 minute. Remove from heat; stir in peanut butter. Add oats and peanuts; stir to mix well. Quickly drop mixture by rounded teaspoonfuls onto wax paper or foil. Cool completely. Store in cool, dry place. *About 4 dozen.*

Tropical Nut Crisps

Thin and crispy, these citrus-flavored cookies are drizzled with melted HERSHEY'S Vanilla Milk Chips.

3/4 cup butter or margarine, softened
1 cup sugar
1/4 cup light corn syrup
1 egg
1/2 teaspoon orange, lemon or pineapple extract
1/2 teaspoon vanilla extract
1 2/3 cups (10-oz. package) HERSHEY'S Vanilla Milk Chips, divided
2 1/2 cups all-purpose flour
2 teaspoons baking soda
1/4 teaspoon salt
1 to 1 1/4 cups ground nuts
VANILLA MILK CHIP GLAZE (recipe follows)

In large mixer bowl, beat butter and sugar until light and fluffy. Add corn syrup, egg, orange and vanilla extracts; blend well. In small microwave-safe bowl, place 1 cup vanilla milk chips. Microwave at HIGH (100%) 1 minute or until smooth when stirred vigorously; blend into butter mixture. In separate bowl, stir together flour, baking soda and salt; add to vanilla mixture, blending well. Refrigerate 1 hour or until dough is firm enough to handle. Heat oven to 350°F. Roll dough into 1-inch balls; roll in nuts, pressing nuts into dough lightly. Place on ungreased cookie sheet. Bake 8 to 10 minutes or until golden around edges. Cool several minutes; remove from cookie sheet to wire rack. Cool completely. Drizzle VANILLA MILK CHIP GLAZE over each cookie. *About 5 dozen cookies.*

VANILLA MILK CHIP GLAZE: In small microwave-safe bowl, place remaining 2/3 cup vanilla milk chips and 1 1/2 teaspoons shortening. Microwave at HIGH (100%) 1 minute; stir until smooth when stirred.

Top to Bottom: Chocolate Chunk Blondies, recipe page 67; Cocoa Oatmeal Treats, Tropical Nut Crisps, recipes page 66.

Chocolate Chunk Blondies

3/4 cup (1 1/2 sticks) butter or
    margarine
1 cup packed light brown sugar
1/2 cup granulated sugar
2 eggs
2 tablespoons milk
2 teaspoons vanilla extract
2 cups all-purpose flour
1 teaspoon baking soda
1/2 teaspoon salt
1/2 cup coarsely chopped nuts
    (optional)
1 3/4 cups (10-oz. package)
    HERSHEY'S Premium
    Semi-Sweet Chocolate Chunks

Heat oven to 350°F. Grease 13 × 9 × 2-inch baking pan. In large mixer bowl, beat butter and sugars until light and fluffy. Add eggs, milk and vanilla; beat well. In separate bowl, stir together flour, baking soda and salt; add to butter mixture. Stir in nuts, if desired, and chocolate chunks; spread into prepared pan. Bake 30 to 35 minutes or until golden brown. Cool completely in pan on wire rack. Cut into bars. *About 36 bars.*

Scrumptious Chocolate Fruit and Nut Cookies ▼

1 1/4 cups (2 1/2 sticks) butter or
     margarine, softened
  2 cups sugar
  2 eggs
  2 teaspoons vanilla extract
  2 cups all-purpose flour
 3/4 cup HERSHEY'S Cocoa
  1 teaspoon baking soda
 1/2 teaspoon salt
  2 cups (12-oz. package)
     HERSHEY'S Semi-Sweet
     Chocolate Chips OR 1 3/4 cups
     (10-oz. package) HERSHEY'S
     Semi-Sweet Chocolate Chunks
  1 cup chopped dried apricots
  1 cup coarsely chopped
     macadamia nuts

Heat oven to 350°F. In large mixer bowl, beat butter and sugar until light and fluffy. Add eggs and vanilla; beat well. In separate bowl, stir together flour, cocoa, baking soda and salt; blend into butter mixture. Stir in chocolate chips, apricots and nuts. Using ice cream scoop or 1/4-cup measuring cup, drop dough onto ungreased cookie sheet. Bake 12 to 14 minutes or until set. Cool slightly; remove from cookie sheet to wire rack. Cool completely. *About 2 dozen 3 1/2-inch cookies.*

Peanut Butter Crisps ▼

  1 cup (2 sticks) butter or
     margarine, softened and
     divided
  1 cup sugar
 1/4 cup light corn syrup
  1 egg
  1 teaspoon vanilla extract
1 2/3 cups (10-oz. package)
     REESE'S Peanut Butter Chips
  2 cups all-purpose flour
  2 teaspoons baking soda
 1/4 teaspoon salt
     Granulated sugar

In large mixer bowl, beat together 3/4 cup butter and sugar until light and fluffy. Add corn syrup, egg and vanilla; blend well. In medium microwave-safe bowl, place peanut butter chips and remaining 1/4 cup butter. Microwave at HIGH (100%) 1 to 1 1/2 minutes; stir until smooth when stirred. Blend into butter mixture. In separate bowl, stir together flour, baking soda and salt; add to peanut butter mixture, blending well. Refrigerate 1 hour or until firm enough to handle. Heat oven to 350°F. Roll dough into 1-inch balls; roll in sugar. Place on ungreased cookie sheet. Bake 10 to 12 minutes or until golden brown around the edges. Cool slightly; remove from cookie sheet to wire rack. Cool completely. *About 5 dozen cookies.*

Pineapple and Vanilla Chip Drops ▼

- 1 cup (2 sticks) butter or margarine, softened
- 1 cup sugar
- 2 eggs
- 1/2 teaspoon vanilla extract
- 1 can (8 oz.) crushed pineapple, with juice
- 3 1/2 cups all-purpose flour
- 1 teaspoon baking soda
- 3/4 teaspoon ground cinnamon
- 1/2 teaspoon salt
- 1/4 teaspoon ground nutmeg
- 1 cup chopped pecans
- 1 2/3 cups (10-oz. package) HERSHEY'S Vanilla Milk Chips

Heat oven to 350°F. Lightly grease cookie sheets. In large mixer bowl, beat butter and sugar until well blended. Add eggs and vanilla; blend thoroughly. Blend in pineapple and juice; blend thoroughly. In small bowl, stir together flour, baking soda, cinnamon, salt and nutmeg. Gradually add to butter mixture, mixing well. Stir in pecans and vanilla milk chips. Drop by tablespoonfuls onto prepared cookie sheet. Bake 10 to 12 minutes or until lightly browned around edges. Remove from cookie sheet to wire rack. Cool completely. *About 5 dozen cookies.*

Peppermint Pattie Cookies ▼

- 2/3 cup butter or margarine, softened
- 1 cup sugar
- 1 egg
- 1/2 teaspoon vanilla extract
- 1 1/2 cups all-purpose flour
- 1/3 cup HERSHEY'S Cocoa
- 1/2 teaspoon baking soda
- 1/4 teaspoon salt
- 1 tablespoon milk
- 12 to 14 small (1 1/2-inch) YORK Peppermint Patties

In large mixer bowl, beat butter and sugar; add egg and vanilla, blending well. In separate bowl, stir together flour, cocoa, baking soda and salt. Add to butter mixture alternately with milk, blending well. Refrigerate dough about 1 hour or until firm enough to handle. (Dough will be a little soft.) Lightly grease cookie sheet. Heat oven to 350°F. Shape small portion of dough around unwrapped peppermint pattie, completely covering candy. Place on prepared cookie sheet; flatten slightly and crimp with tines of fork around edge, if desired. Bake 10 to 12 minutes or until set. Cool 1 minute; remove from cookie sheet to wire rack. Cool completely. *About 12 to 14 cookies.*

▲ *Chocolate Oatmeal Cookies*

These chewy chocolate oatmeal cookies are a change of pace from traditional oatmeal cookies.

1 **cup (2 sticks) butter or margarine, softened**
1 1/2 **cups granulated sugar**
1 **cup packed light brown sugar**
2 **eggs**
2 **teaspoons vanilla extract**
1 1/2 **cups all-purpose flour**
1/2 **cup HERSHEY'S Cocoa**
1 **teaspoon baking soda**
1/2 **teaspoon salt**
3 **cups quick-cooking or regular rolled oats**
1/2 **cup chopped nuts**

Heat oven to 350°F. In large mixer bowl, beat butter and sugars until light and fluffy; blend in eggs and vanilla. In separate bowl, stir together flour, cocoa, baking soda and salt; gradually add to butter mixture, mixing well. Stir in oats and nuts. (Batter will be stiff.) Drop by rounded tablespoonfuls onto ungreased cookie sheet. Bake 11 to 12 minutes or until set; cookies will be slightly moist in center. DO NOT OVERBAKE. Cool 1 minute; remove from cookie sheet to wire rack. Cool completely. *About 4 dozen cookies.*

Pecan-Topped ◄ Chocolate Cookies

2/3 cup butter or margarine
3/4 cup sugar
1 egg
1 1/2 teaspoons vanilla extract
1 1/3 cups all-purpose flour
1/3 cup HERSHEY'S Cocoa
1/4 teaspoon baking powder
1/4 teaspoon baking soda
1/8 teaspoon salt
About 48 pecan halves
CHOCOLATE GLAZE (recipe follows)

In large mixer bowl, beat butter, sugar, egg and vanilla until light and fluffy. In separate bowl, stir together flour, cocoa, baking powder, baking soda and salt; add to butter mixture, beating until well blended. Cover; refrigerate about 1 hour. Heat oven to 350°F. Shape dough into 1-inch balls. Place on ungreased cookie sheet. Bake 8 to 10 minutes or until almost set. Remove from cookie sheet to wire rack. Cool completely. Frost with CHOCOLATE GLAZE; top each cookie with pecan half. *About 4 dozen cookies.*

CHOCOLATE GLAZE: In small saucepan, stir together 2 tablespoons sugar and 2 tablespoons water. Cook over medium heat, stirring constantly until mixture boils and sugar is dissolved. Remove from heat; immediately add 1/2 cup HERSHEY'S Semi-Sweet Chocolate Chips, stirring until melted. Cool to spreading consistency. *About 1/2 cup glaze.*

REESE'S Peanut Blossoms

These cookies may be different from ones you have made before because these use peanut butter chips for a rich peanut flavor.

1/2 cup (1 stick) butter or margarine
1 cup REESE'S Peanut Butter Chips
2/3 cup packed light brown sugar
1 egg
3/4 teaspoon vanilla extract
1 1/3 cups all-purpose flour
3/4 teaspoon baking soda
1/2 cup finely chopped nuts
Granulated sugar
1 bag (9 oz.) HERSHEY'S KISSES Chocolates, unwrapped

Heat oven to 350°F. In saucepan over low heat, place butter and peanut butter chips; heat, stirring constantly, until melted. Pour mixture into large mixer bowl; add brown sugar, egg and vanilla, beating until well blended. Stir in flour, baking soda and nuts, blending well. Shape dough into 1-inch balls. Roll in granulated sugar; place on ungreased cookie sheet. Bake 10 to 12 minutes or until lightly browned. Immediately place unwrapped chocolate piece on top of each cookie, pressing down so cookie cracks around edges. Remove from cookie sheet to wire rack. Cool completely. *About 4 dozen cookies.*

BAKER'S TIPS

Homemade cookies are a favorite for everyone. Here are a few hints to make your cookies perfect every time.

• Do not grease the cookie sheet unless it is called for in the recipe.

• Make cookies in each batch the same size to ensure even baking.

• Bake one sheet at a time in the center of the oven for evenly browned cookies.

• Check cookies at minimum baking time given. Underbaking results in soft, doughy cookies and overbaking results in dry, hard cookies.

• Completely cool cookies in a single layer on a wire rack before storing.

BROWNIES & BARS

Fill picnic baskets, lunch boxes, hungry tummies and more with love and good taste. Your family will savor these delicious treasures at lunchtime, snacktime, anytime. They're all fun to bake . . . and even more fun to eat! Family and friends will relish the indulgent taste — you'll be pleased you baked them yourself.

Clockwise from Left: English Toffee Bars, recipe page 83; Peanut Butter Marble Brownies, recipe page 78; Chocolate Cream Cheese Brownies, recipe page 76.

Creamy Filled Brownies

1/2 cup (1 stick) butter or margarine
1/3 cup HERSHEY'S Cocoa
2 eggs
1 cup sugar
1/2 cup all-purpose flour
1/4 teaspoon baking powder
1/4 teaspoon salt
1 teaspoon vanilla extract
1 cup finely chopped nuts
CREAMY FILLING (recipe follows)
MINI CHIP GLAZE (recipe follows)
1/2 cup chopped nuts (optional)

Heat oven to 350°F. Line 15 1/2 × 10 1/2 × 1-inch jelly roll pan with foil; grease foil. In small saucepan, melt butter; remove from heat. Stir in cocoa until smooth. In small mixer bowl, beat eggs; gradually add sugar, beating until fluffy. In separate bowl, stir together flour, baking powder and salt; add to egg mixture. Add cocoa mixture and vanilla; blend well. Stir in 1 cup nuts. Spread batter in prepared pan. Bake 12 to 14 minutes or until top springs back when touched lightly in center. Cool completely in pan on wire rack; remove from pan to cutting board. Remove foil; cut brownie in half crosswise. Spread one half with CREAMY FILLING; top with second half. Glaze with MINI CHIP GLAZE; sprinkle with remaining nuts. After glaze has set, cut into bars. *About 24 bars.*

CREAMY FILLING: In small bowl, combine 1 package (3 ounces) softened cream cheese, 2 tablespoons softened butter or margarine and 1 teaspoon vanilla extract. Gradually add 1 1/2 cups powdered sugar; beat to spreading consistency.

MINI CHIP GLAZE: In small saucepan, heat 1/4 cup sugar and 2 tablespoons water to boiling. Remove from heat. Immediately add 1/2 cup HERSHEY'S MINI CHIPS Semi-Sweet Chocolate, stirring until melted.

Cherry-Bright Chocolate Brownies

This is a very moist, tender and light brownie filled with cherries.

1/2 cup chopped maraschino cherries, well drained
1/3 cup butter or margarine, softened
3/4 cup sugar
2 eggs
2 tablespoons light corn syrup
1 teaspoon almond extract OR 2 tablespoons kirsch (cherry brandy)
1 teaspoon vanilla extract
2/3 cup all-purpose flour
1/3 cup HERSHEY'S Cocoa
1/2 teaspoon salt
1/4 teaspoon baking powder
1/3 cup chopped slivered almonds
Additional maraschino cherries, quartered (optional)

Heat oven to 350°F. Grease and flour 9-inch square baking pan. Blot cherries between paper towels to remove excess moisture; set aside. In small mixer bowl, beat butter, sugar and eggs; blend in corn syrup, almond extract and vanilla. Add flour, cocoa, salt and baking powder; blend until combined. Stir in cherries and almonds; pour into prepared pan. Bake 25 to 30 minutes or until brownies begin to pull away from sides of pan. Cool completely in pan on wire rack. Frost, if desired. Cut into squares. Garnish with additional maraschino cherries, if desired. *About 16 brownies.*

Top to Bottom: Cherry-Bright Chocolate Brownies, recipe page 74; Peanutty Chewy Bars, recipe page 75; Creamy Filled Brownies, recipe page 74.

Peanutty Chewy Bars

1¹/₄ cups all-purpose flour
²/₃ cup granulated sugar
¹/₃ cup HERSHEY'S Cocoa
¹/₄ cup packed light brown sugar
1 teaspoon baking powder
¹/₄ teaspoon salt
¹/₂ cup (1 stick) butter or margarine
2 eggs, slightly beaten
1²/₃ cups (10-oz. package) REESE'S Peanut Butter Chips
1 can (14 oz.) sweetened condensed milk
1 cup flaked coconut

Heat oven to 350°F. Grease 13 × 9 × 2-inch baking pan. In large bowl, stir together flour, granulated sugar, cocoa, brown sugar, baking powder and salt. Add butter; cut in with pastry blender or with hands until mixture is well blended, resembling coarse crumbs. Add eggs; mix well. Spoon mixture into prepared pan, pressing firmly onto bottom of pan. Bake 8 to 10 minutes or until mixture is set. Remove from oven; sprinkle peanut butter chips on top. Drizzle sweetened condensed milk evenly over chips; top with coconut. Return to oven; bake 20 to 25 minutes or until lightly browned on top. Cool completely in pan on wire rack. Cut into bars. *About 24 bars.*

Chocolate Cream Cheese Brownies

Rich and fudgey, cream cheese adds extra moisture to these brownies.

- 1 **cup (2 sticks) butter or margarine, softened**
- 1 **package (3 oz.) cream cheese, softened**
- 2 **cups sugar**
- 3 **eggs**
- 1 **teaspoon vanilla extract**
- 1 **cup all-purpose flour**
- 3/4 **cup HERSHEY'S Cocoa**
- 1/4 **teaspoon baking powder**
- 1/2 **teaspoon salt**
- 3/4 **cup chopped nuts**
  BROWNIE FROSTING

Heat oven to 325°F. Grease bottom of 13 × 9 × 2-inch baking pan. In large mixer bowl, beat butter, cream cheese and sugar until light and fluffy. Beat in eggs and vanilla. In separate bowl, stir together flour, cocoa, baking powder and salt; gradually add to butter mixture until well blended. Stir in nuts. Spread batter evenly in prepared pan. Bake 35 to 40 minutes or just until brownies begin to pull away from sides of pan. Cool completely. Frost with BROWNIE FROSTING. Cut into bars. *About 36 brownies.*

BROWNIE FROSTING

- 3 **tablespoons butter or margarine, softened**
- 3 **tablespoons HERSHEY'S Cocoa**
- 3/4 **teaspoon vanilla extract**
- 1 1/3 **cups powdered sugar**
- 1 **to 2 tablespoons milk**
- 1 **tablespoon light corn syrup (optional)**

In small mixer bowl, beat butter and cocoa; add vanilla and powdered sugar. Blend in milk and corn syrup, if desired; beat to spreading consistency. *1 cup frosting.*

Cocoa Raisin-Nut Brownie Bars ▼

- 1/2 **cup (1 stick) butter or margarine, softened**
- 1 **cup sugar**
- 2 **eggs**
- 1 **teaspoon vanilla extract**
- 1/2 **cup all-purpose flour**
- 1/2 **cup HERSHEY'S Premium European Style Cocoa**
- 1/2 **cup HERSHEY'S Semi-Sweet Chocolate Chips**
- 1/2 **cup raisins or golden raisins**
- 1/2 **cup coarsely chopped nuts**
- 1/4 **to 1/2 teaspoon ground cinnamon**
- 1/8 **teaspoon salt**
  Powdered sugar (optional)

Heat oven to 350°F. Grease 8-inch square baking pan. In small mixer bowl, beat butter, sugar, eggs and vanilla until light and fluffy. In separate bowl, stir together flour, cocoa, chocolate chips, raisins, nuts, cinnamon and salt; add to butter mixture, stirring until well blended. Spread batter into prepared pan. Bake 30 to 35 minutes or until bars just begin to pull away from sides of pan; cool completely in pan on wire rack. Cut into bars. Sift powdered sugar over top, if desired. *About 20 bars.*

Peanut Butter Chip Brownies ▼

- 3/4 cup (1 1/2 sticks) butter or margarine
- 1 cup sugar
- 1/4 cup light corn syrup
- 1 teaspoon vanilla extract
- 2 eggs
- 1 1/4 cups all-purpose flour
- 1/2 cup HERSHEY'S Cocoa
- 1/2 teaspoon baking powder
- 1/4 teaspoon salt
- 1 1/2 cups REESE'S Peanut Butter Chips

Heat oven to 350°F. Grease 13 × 9 × 2-inch baking pan. In large mixer bowl, beat butter, sugar, corn syrup and vanilla until light and fluffy. Add eggs, one at a time, beating until well blended. In separate bowl, stir together flour, cocoa, baking powder and salt; gradually blend into butter mixture. Stir in peanut butter chips. Spread into prepared pan. Bake 20 to 25 minutes or until brownies just begin to pull away from sides of pan. Cool completely in pan on wire rack. Cut into bars. *About 36 brownies.*

HERSHEY'S Premium Doubly Chocolate Brownies ▼

- 3/4 cup HERSHEY'S Cocoa
- 1/2 teaspoon baking soda
- 2/3 cup butter or margarine, melted and divided
- 1/2 cup boiling water
- 2 cups sugar
- 2 eggs
- 1 1/3 cups all-purpose flour
- 1 teaspoon vanilla extract
- 1/4 teaspoon salt
- 1/2 cup coarsely chopped nuts (optional)
- 1 3/4 cups (10-oz. package) HERSHEY'S Premium Semi-Sweet Chocolate Chunks

Heat oven to 350°F. Grease 13 × 9 × 2-inch baking pan. In large bowl, stir together cocoa and baking soda; blend in 1/3 cup butter. Add boiling water; stir until mixture thickens. Stir in sugar, eggs and remaining 1/3 cup butter; stir until smooth. Add flour, vanilla and salt; blend well. Stir in nuts, if desired, and chocolate chunks. Pour into prepared pan. Bake 35 to 40 minutes or until brownies begin to pull away from sides of pan. Cool completely in pan on wire rack. Cut into squares. *About 36 brownies.*

Peanut Butter Marble Brownies

1/2 cup (1 stick) butter or margarine
1/3 cup HERSHEY'S Cocoa
3 eggs
1 1/4 cups sugar, divided
1 teaspoon vanilla extract
1/2 cup all-purpose flour
1/2 teaspoon baking powder
1/4 teaspoon salt
1 cup REESE'S Peanut Butter Chips, divided
1 package (3 oz.) cream cheese, softened

Heat oven to 350°F. Grease 9-inch square baking pan. In small saucepan, melt butter; remove from heat. Stir in cocoa, blending well; set aside. In small mixer bowl, beat 2 eggs until foamy; gradually add 1 cup sugar and vanilla, blending well. In separate bowl, stir together flour, baking powder and salt; blend into egg mixture. Add cocoa mixture and 1/2 cup peanut butter chips; blend well. Remove 1/2 cup batter; set aside. Spread remaining batter in prepared pan. In microwave-safe bowl, place remaining 1/2 cup peanut butter chips. Microwave at HIGH (100%) 30 seconds or until chips are melted when stirred. In small mixer bowl, combine cream cheese, remaining 1/4 cup sugar and melted peanut butter chips; beat until smooth. Add remaining egg; blend well. Spread cream cheese mixture over chocolate batter. Drop reserved 1/2 cup chocolate batter by spoonfuls onto cream cheese layer. With knife, gently swirl top of batter into cream cheese layer for marbled effect. Bake 40 to 45 minutes or just until brownies begin to pull away from sides of pan. Cool completely in pan on wire rack. Cut into squares. *About 16 brownies.*

Mississippi Mud Brownies

4 eggs
1 1/2 cups sugar
1 1/2 teaspoons vanilla extract
1 1/2 cups all-purpose flour
1/2 cup HERSHEY'S Cocoa
1/8 teaspoon salt
1 cup (2 sticks) butter or margarine, melted
1 cup chopped pecans
1 jar (7 oz.) marshmallow creme
ONE-BOWL BUTTERCREAM FROSTING (recipe follows)

Heat oven to 350°F. Grease and flour 13 × 9 × 2-inch baking pan. In large mixer bowl, beat eggs until foamy. Gradually beat in sugar and vanilla. In separate bowl, stir together flour, cocoa and salt; add alternately with butter to egg mixture. Blend well. Stir in pecans. Pour batter into prepared pan. Bake 25 to 30 minutes or until wooden pick inserted in center comes out clean. Immediately spread marshmallow creme gently over top. Spread frosting gently over warm marshmallow creme; swirl lightly for marbled effect. Cool completely. *About 24 brownies.*

ONE-BOWL BUTTERCREAM FROSTING

3 tablespoons butter or margarine, softened
1 cup powdered sugar
1/4 cup HERSHEY'S Cocoa
2 to 3 tablespoons milk
1/2 teaspoon vanilla extract

In small mixer bowl, beat butter. Add powdered sugar and cocoa alternately with milk; beat to spreading consistency. Blend in vanilla. *About 1 cup frosting.*

Rocky Road Brownies (front left), recipe page 79, Mississippi Mud Brownies (front right), recipe page 78.

Rocky Road Brownies

1 cup HERSHEY'S Semi-Sweet
   Chocolate Chips
1¼ cups miniature marshmallows
1 cup chopped nuts
½ cup (1 stick) butter or
   margarine
1 cup sugar
1 teaspoon vanilla extract
2 eggs
½ cup all-purpose flour
⅓ cup HERSHEY'S Cocoa
½ teaspoon baking powder
½ teaspoon salt

Heat oven to 350°F. Grease 9-inch square baking pan. Stir together chocolate chips, marshmallows and nuts; set aside. In large microwave-safe bowl, place butter. Microwave at HIGH (100% power) 1 to 1½ minutes or until melted. Add sugar, vanilla and eggs, beating with spoon until well blended. Add flour, cocoa, baking powder and salt; blend well. Spread batter into prepared pan. Bake 22 minutes. Sprinkle chocolate chip mixture over top. Continue baking 5 minutes or until marshmallows have softened and puffed slightly. Cool completely. With wet knife, cut into squares.
About 20 brownies.

HERSHEY'S Best Brownies

These easy-to-make, rich and moist brownies are our best, and we've made the recipe especially easy-to-make by using only one bowl.

1 cup (2 sticks) butter or
   margarine
2 cups sugar
2 teaspoons vanilla extract
4 eggs
¾ cup HERSHEY'S Premium
   European Style Cocoa or
   HERSHEY'S Cocoa
1 cup all-purpose flour
½ teaspoon baking powder
¼ teaspoon salt
1 cup chopped nuts (optional)

Heat oven to 350°F. Grease 13 × 9 × 2-inch baking pan. In large microwave-safe bowl, place butter. Microwave at HIGH (100%) 2 to 2½ minutes or until melted. Stir in sugar and vanilla. Add eggs, one at a time, beating well with wooden spoon after each addition. Add cocoa; beat until well blended. Add flour, baking powder and salt; beat well. Stir in nuts, if desired. Pour batter into prepared pan. Bake 30 to 35 minutes or until brownies just begin to pull away from sides of pan. Cool in pan on wire rack. Cut into bars.
About 36 brownies.

Vanilla Chip Lemon Bars

1 1/4 cups all-purpose flour, divided
1 cup granulated sugar, divided
1/3 cup margarine, softened
3/4 cup HERSHEY'S Vanilla Milk Chips
1/2 cup frozen egg substitute, thawed
1/4 cup lemon juice
2 teaspoons grated lemon peel
Powdered sugar

Heat oven to 350°F. In medium bowl, stir together 1 cup flour and 1/4 cup granulated sugar; with pastry blender, cut in margarine until mixture resembles coarse crumbs. Press mixture onto bottom of 9-inch square baking pan. Bake 15 minutes or until lightly browned. Remove from oven; sprinkle vanilla chips over crust. In medium bowl, stir together egg substitute, lemon juice, lemon peel, remaining 1/4 cup flour and remaining 3/4 cup sugar; carefully pour over chips and crust. Bake 15 minutes or until set. Cool slightly in pan on wire rack; sprinkle with powdered sugar. Cool completely. Cut into bars. *About 3 dozen bars.*

Almond MINI CHIP Shortbread

Flavored with almond, this MINI CHIP studded cookie is perfect for serving with tea.

1 cup (2 sticks) butter, softened
1/2 cup sugar
2 1/2 cups all-purpose flour
1 teaspoon almond extract
1 cup HERSHEY'S MINI CHIPS Semi-Sweet Chocolate

Heat oven to 350°F. Grease 13 × 9 × 2-inch baking pan. In large mixer bowl, beat butter and sugar until light and fluffy. Add flour and almond extract; blend well. Stir in small chocolate chips; pat into prepared pan. Bake 30 minutes or until golden brown. Cool in pan on wire rack 10 minutes. Cut into bars. Cool completely in pan on wire rack. *About 36 bars.*

Chippy Chewy Bars

1/2 cup (1 stick) butter or margarine
1 1/2 cups graham cracker crumbs
1 2/3 cups (10-oz. package) REESE'S Peanut Butter Chips, divided
1 1/2 cups flaked coconut
1 can (14 oz.) sweetened condensed milk
1 cup HERSHEY'S Semi-Sweet Chocolate Chips
1 1/2 teaspoons shortening

Heat oven to 350°F. Place butter in 13 × 9 × 2-inch baking pan; place in oven until melted. Remove pan from oven; sprinkle crumbs evenly over butter and press down with fork. Layer 1 cup peanut butter chips over crumbs; sprinkle coconut over peanut butter chips. Layer remaining 2/3 cup peanut butter chips over coconut; drizzle sweetened condensed milk evenly over top. Bake 20 minutes or until lightly browned. Remove from oven. In small microwave-safe bowl, place chocolate chips and shortening. Microwave at HIGH (100%) 1 to 1 1/2 minutes or until chips are melted when stirred. Drizzle evenly over bars. Cool completely in pan on wire rack. Cut into bars. *About 4 dozen bars.*

Almond Chocolate Cookie Bars

- 1 cup (2 sticks) butter or margarine
- 1/2 cup granulated sugar
- 1/2 cup packed light brown sugar
- 1 egg yolk
- 1 teaspoon vanilla extract
- 2 cups all-purpose flour
- 1 1/2 cups HERSHEY'S MINI CHIPS Semi-Sweet Chocolate
- 3/4 cup sliced almonds, chopped or pecans

Heat oven to 350°F. In large mixer bowl, beat butter with sugars until fluffy; beat in egg yolk and vanilla. Stir in flour; pat into ungreased 13 × 9 × 2-inch baking pan. Bake 25 to 30 minutes or until lightly browned. Remove from oven; cool 5 minutes. Sprinkle with small chocolate chips. As chocolate melts, spread to cover entire crust. Sprinkle with nuts; press lightly into chocolate. Cool in pan on wire rack. Cut into bars. *About 36 bars.*

Left to Right: Vanilla Chip Lemon Bars, Chippy Chewy Bars, recipes page 80; Almond Chocolate Cookie Bars, recipe page 81.

Almond MINI CHIP Shortbread (left), recipe page 80; Chocolate Chunk Raspberry Bars (right), recipe page 82.

Chocolate Chunk Raspberry Bars

1/3 cup sugar
2 tablespoons butter or margarine
2 tablespoons water
1 3/4 cups (10-oz. package) HERSHEY'S Premium Semi-Sweet Chocolate Chunks, divided
1 egg
1 teaspoon vanilla extract
2/3 cup all-purpose flour
1/4 teaspoon baking powder
1/4 teaspoon salt
1/3 cup seedless raspberry preserves
1/2 cup finely chopped nuts
   Pecan halves (optional)

Heat oven to 350°F. Grease 8-inch square baking pan. In medium saucepan, combine sugar, butter and water. Cook over medium heat, stirring constantly, until mixture boils. Remove from heat; immediately add 1 cup chocolate chunks, stirring until melted. Stir in egg and vanilla until blended. In separate bowl, stir together flour, baking powder and salt; add to chocolate mixture. Stir in remaining 3/4 cup chocolate chunks; spread into prepared pan. Place pan in freezer 10 minutes. Stir raspberry preserves to soften; spread over chilled batter. Sprinkle chopped nuts over top. Bake 35 to 40 minutes or until brownies begin to pull away from sides of pan. Cool completely in pan on wire rack. Cut into bars. Garnish with pecan halves, if desired. *About 16 bars.*

Fudgey Chocolate Cookie Bars

1³/4 cups all-purpose flour
³/4 cup powdered sugar
1/4 cup HERSHEY'S Cocoa
1 cup (2 sticks) cold butter or margarine
2 cups (12-oz. package) HERSHEY'S Semi-Sweet Chocolate Chips, divided
1 can (14 oz.) sweetened condensed milk
1 teaspoon vanilla extract
1 cup chopped nuts

Heat oven to 350°F. In medium bowl, stir together flour, sugar and cocoa; cut in butter until crumbly (mixture will be dry). Press firmly on bottom of 13 × 9 × 2-inch baking pan. Bake 15 minutes. Meanwhile, in medium saucepan, combine 1 cup chocolate chips, sweetened condensed milk and vanilla. Cook over medium heat, stirring constantly, until chips are melted. Pour evenly over prepared crust. Top with nuts and remaining 1 cup chips; press down firmly. Bake 20 minutes or until set. Cool in pan on wire rack. Refrigerate, if desired. Cut into bars. Store tightly covered. *About 2 dozen bars.*

English Toffee Bars

English toffee is traditionally made by boiling sugar and butter together to make a rich, brown, sugar-flavored confection. That flavor is incorporated in this cookie bar topped with chocolate.

2 cups all-purpose flour
1 cup packed light brown sugar
1/2 cup (1 stick) butter
1 cup pecan halves
    TOFFEE TOPPING (recipe follows)
1 cup HERSHEY'S Milk Chocolate Chips

Heat oven to 350°F. In large mixer bowl, combine flour, brown sugar and butter; mix until fine crumbs form. (A few large crumbs may remain.) Press into ungreased 13 × 9 × 2-inch baking pan. Sprinkle pecans over crust. Prepare TOFFEE TOPPING; drizzle evenly over pecans and crust. Bake 20 to 22 minutes or until topping is bubbly and golden; remove from oven. Immediately sprinkle milk chocolate chips over top; press gently onto surface. Cool completely in pan on wire rack. Cut into bars. *About 3 dozen bars.*

TOFFEE TOPPING: In small saucepan over medium heat, combine ²/3 cup butter and 1/3 cup packed light brown sugar; cook, stirring constantly, until mixture comes to boil. Continue boiling, stirring constantly, 30 seconds; use immediately.

BAKER'S TIPS

• When cookies DO NOT spread, the dough might be overmixed or the oven temperature was too hot. Always use an oven thermometer.
• When cookies spread TOO MUCH, the oven temperature might be too cool or the cookie sheet was greased too heavily.

LIGHTER DESSERTS

If your family loves the inviting taste and texture of chocolate — but you want to provide lighter treats — consider the sweet options in this chapter. These delights have all the irresistible taste of chocolate without excess fat, calories and cholesterol.

Lighter Than Air Chocolate Almond Parfaits (top), recipe page 89; Fruit-Filled Chocolate Dreams (bottom), recipe page 88.

Chocolate Yogurt Creme Pudding

This pudding is low in fat, but rich in flavor. Although you can't taste the yogurt, the rich velvety texture comes from the wholesomeness of yogurt.

1 cup sugar
1/3 cup HERSHEY'S Cocoa
1 envelope unflavored gelatin
1 1/3 cups 2% lowfat milk
2 cups vanilla lowfat yogurt
1 teaspoon vanilla extract
Raspberries or sliced fresh strawberries

In medium saucepan, stir together sugar, cocoa and gelatin. Gradually stir in milk; let stand 5 minutes. Cook over medium heat, stirring constantly, until mixture comes to a boil and gelatin is dissolved. Cool slightly. Add yogurt and vanilla; blend gently just until well combined. Pour into dessert dishes. Refrigerate 6 hours or until set. Top with fruit. *8 servings.*

Nutrition Information Per Serving:

Calories	170	Cholesterol, mg	5
Protein, gm	6	Sodium, mg	65
Carbohydrates, gm	33	Calcium, mg	160
Fat, gm	2		

Clockwise from Top: Chocolate Yogurt Creme Pudding, recipe page 87; Choco-Orange Fluff, recipe page 88; Chocolate-Filled Meringue Shells, recipe page 87.

BAKER'S TIP

Chocolate lovers do not have to sacrifice their favorite flavor when they follow a low-calorie eating plan. Savory chocolate sweets can be part of the diet when they are made with HERSHEY'S Cocoa, a deep, dark chocolate baking ingredient that's naturally low in fat (12% by weight) and very low in sodium and cholesterol.

Chocolate-Filled Meringue Shells with Strawberry Sauce

Delicate in flavor and color, these meringue shells are easy to make. The crisp texture of the meringue is a perfect complement to the creamy chocolate filling.

2 egg whites
1/4 teaspoon cream of tartar
Dash salt
1/2 cup sugar
1/4 teaspoon vanilla extract
CHOCOLATE FILLING (recipe follows)
1 package (10 oz.) frozen strawberries in syrup, thawed

Heat oven to 275°F. Paper-line 12 muffin cups (2 1/2 inches in diameter). In small mixer bowl, beat egg whites with cream of tartar and salt until soft peaks form. Beat in sugar, 1 tablespoon at a time, until stiff, glossy peaks form. Stir in vanilla. Spoon 2 1/2 to 3 tablespoons meringue in each prepared cup. Using back of spoon or small spatula, push meringue up sides of paper cups forming well in center. Bake 1 hour or until meringue turns delicate cream color and feels dry to the touch. Cool in pan on wire rack. Spoon CHOCOLATE FILLING into shells. Before serving, carefully remove paper from shells. Purée strawberries; spoon over meringues. Refrigerate leftovers. *12 servings.*

CHOCOLATE FILLING: In small mixer bowl, beat 1 package (8 oz.) softened Neufchâtel cheese (light cream cheese) and 1/4 cup HERSHEY'S Cocoa. Gradually add 1 cup powdered sugar, beating until well blended. Fold in 1 cup frozen non-dairy whipped topping, thawed.

Nutrition Information Per Serving:

Calories	160	Cholesterol, mg	15
Protein, gm	3	Sodium, mg	105
Carbohydrates, gm	24	Calcium, mg	20
Fat, gm	6		

Choco-Orange Fluff

Flavorful, yet light and fluffy, this low-calorie dessert is pretty served in wine glasses.

  1 **envelope unflavored gelatin**
  1/3 **cup sugar**
  1/4 **cup HERSHEY'S Cocoa**
  2 **cups skim milk**
  1 **teaspoon vanilla extract**
  1/8 **to** 1/4 **teaspoon orange extract**
1 1/2 **cups frozen non-dairy**
    whipped topping, thawed
    Whipped topping (optional)
    Fresh orange wedges
    (optional)

In medium saucepan, stir together gelatin, sugar and cocoa. Stir in milk; let stand 2 minutes to soften. Cook over medium heat, stirring constantly, until gelatin is completely dissolved, about 5 minutes. Pour mixture into medium bowl; stir in vanilla and orange extracts. Refrigerate, stirring occasionally, until mixture mounds slightly when dropped from spoon. Add whipped topping to chocolate mixture; beat with wire whisk until well blended. Spoon into dessert dishes. Refrigerate 3 to 4 hours or until set. Garnish with whipped topping and orange wedges, if desired. *Eight 1/2-cup servings.*

Nutrition Information Per Serving:

Calories	110	Cholesterol, mg	0
Protein, gm	4	Sodium, mg	35
Carbohydrates, gm	15	Calcium, mg	80
Fat, gm	4		

BAKER'S TIP

Bloom, the gray-white film that sometimes appears on chocolate bars and chips, occurs when chocolate is exposed to varying temperatures. It does not affect the taste or quality of the chocolate.

Fruit-Filled Chocolate Dreams

As light as pillows, these lowfat puffs may be made ahead of time and frozen. Then simply fill with fruit and serve with the rich chocolate sauce for a dreamy dessert.

  1/2 **cup cold skim milk**
  1/2 **teaspoon vanilla extract**
  1 **envelope (1.3 oz.) whipped**
    topping mix
  1 **tablespoon HERSHEY'S Cocoa**
    Assorted fresh fruit, cut up
    CHOCOLATE SAUCE (recipe
    follows)

Place foil on cookie sheet. In small deep narrow-bottom bowl, blend milk, vanilla, topping mix and cocoa. Whip at high speed of electric mixer until topping peaks, about 2 minutes. Continue beating 2 minutes longer until topping is light and fluffy. Spoon mixture into five mounds onto prepared cookie sheet. With spoon, shape into 4-inch shells. Freeze. To serve, fill center of each frozen shell with fruit; drizzle with CHOCOLATE SAUCE. Serve immediately. *5 servings.*

CHOCOLATE SAUCE

  3/4 **cup sugar**
  1/3 **cup HERSHEY'S Cocoa**
  1 **tablespoon cornstarch**
  3/4 **cup water**
  1 **tablespoon margarine**
  1 **teaspoon vanilla extract**

In small saucepan, combine sugar, cocoa and cornstarch; stir in water. Cook over medium heat, stirring constantly, until mixture comes to a boil; boil 1 minute. Remove from heat; add margarine and vanilla, stirring until smooth. Refrigerate thoroughly. *About 1 cup sauce.*

Nutrition Information Per Serving:

Calories	154	Cholesterol, mg	0
Protein, gm	2	Sodium, mg	31
Carbohydrates, gm	29	Calcium, mg	11
Fat, gm	2		

Lighter Than Air Chocolate Almond Parfaits

1 cup sugar, divided
1/3 cup plus 1 tablespoon water, divided
1 container (8 oz.) frozen egg substitute, thawed
3 tablespoons all-purpose flour
2 tablespoons reduced-calorie margarine
1/4 cup HERSHEY'S Cocoa or Premium European Style Cocoa
1/2 teaspoon almond extract
2 envelopes (1.3 oz. each) whipped topping mix
1 cup cold skim milk
1 teaspoon vanilla extract

In small saucepan, combine 2/3 cup sugar and 1/3 cup water; cook over medium heat, stirring constantly, until sugar dissolves and mixture boils. Boil, without stirring, 5 minutes; remove from heat. Meanwhile, in large mixer bowl, beat liquid egg substitute until frothy. Gradually add flour, 1 tablespoon at a time, beating thoroughly. Gradually beat hot sugar mixture into egg mixture; continue beating until cool, about 5 minutes. In small microwave-safe bowl, stir together margarine, remaining 1 tablespoon water, cocoa and remaining 1/3 cup sugar; microwave at HIGH (100%) 1 to 1 1/2 minutes or until mixture is smooth when stirred. Cool slightly. Pour 1 cup egg mixture into small bowl; stir in almond extract, blending well. Blend chocolate mixture into remaining egg mixture. In large mixer bowl, combine dry whipped topping mix, skim milk and vanilla; beat according to package directions. Remove 1 1/2 cups whipped topping mixture; fold into almond mixture. Fold chocolate mixture into remaining whipped topping mixture. Divide half of almond mixture evenly among 11 parfait or wine glasses; top with half of chocolate mixture. Layer remaining almond mixture over chocolate; finish with remaining chocolate mixture. Cover, freeze until firm,

about 8 hours. Allow to soften at least 5 minutes before serving. *11 servings (about 1/3 cup each).*

Nutrition Information Per Serving:

Calories	170	Cholesterol, mg	0
Protein, gm	4	Sodium, mg	65
Carbohydrates, gm	28	Calcium, mg	45
Fat, gm	4		

Caribbean Freeze

Make this light chocolate sorbet for a fat-free summer dessert.

2/3 cup sugar
3 tablespoons HERSHEY'S Cocoa
1 3/4 cups water
3 tablespoons frozen pineapple juice concentrate, thawed
1 tablespoon golden rum or 1/2 teaspoon rum extract

In medium saucepan, stir together sugar and cocoa; stir in water. Cook over medium heat, stirring occasionally, until mixture boils; simmer 3 minutes. Cool to room temperature; stir in concentrate and rum. Refrigerate 6 hours or until very cold. Pour cold mixture into 1-quart container of ice cream freezer; freeze according to manufacturer's directions. *About 4 servings.*

Nutrition Information Per Serving:

Calories	165	Cholesterol, mg	0
Protein, gm	1	Sodium, mg	2
Carbohydrates, gm	40	Calcium, mg	11
Fat, gm	0		

BAKER'S TIPS

- Look for recipes specifying skim or lowfat milk. Don't substitute skim milk in recipes just calling for milk because not all recipes will work with lowfat substitutes.
- Don't substitute diet margarine or spreads for butter or regular margarine (again, they may not work).
- Try whipping chilled evaporated skim milk to use as a substitute for a garnish.

Lighter Cocoa Cheesecake

ZWIEBACK CRUST (recipe
follows)
2 packages (8 oz. each) Neufchâtel
cheese (light cream cheese),
softened
3/4 cup sugar
1/3 cup HERSHEY'S Cocoa
1 teaspoon vanilla extract
1/2 cup liquid egg substitute
1 cup vanilla lowfat yogurt
Fresh fruit, sliced

Prepare ZWIEBACK CRUST; set aside.
Heat oven to 350°F. In large mixer
bowl, beat Neufchâtel cheese, sugar,
cocoa and vanilla until light and fluffy.
Add egg substitute; blend well. Pour
into prepared crust; bake 20 minutes.
Remove from oven; cool 15 minutes.
Increase oven temperature to 425°F.
Spread yogurt evenly over top. Bake
10 minutes. Remove from oven to cooling rack. Loosen cheesecake from rim
of pan; cool to room temperature. Refrigerate several hours or overnight;
remove rim of pan. Garnish with fresh
fruit. Cover; refrigerate leftovers.
10 to 12 servings.

ZWIEBACK CRUST: Crush 6 slices
zwieback toast; combine with 1 tablespoon sugar and 1 tablespoon melted
margarine. Press mixture onto bottom of 9-inch springform pan.

Nutrition Information Per Serving:

Calories	240	Cholesterol, mg	40
Protein, gm	8	Sodium, mg	245
Carbohydrates, gm	23	Calcium, mg	85
Fat, gm	13		

BAKER'S TIP

When storing HERSHEY'S
Cocoa, avoid contact with moisture and/or high heat; they could
cause clumping and gray discolor-
ation, although neither affect
cocoa flavor or quality.

Choco-Lite Ladyfinger Dessert

*Ladyfingers are light sponge cake
"fingers." Although they are readily
found in bakeries, strips of angel food
cake could be substituted.*

1 envelope unflavored gelatin
1/2 cup cold water
6 tablespoons sugar
3 tablespoons HERSHEY'S Cocoa
1 1/2 cups skim milk
2 egg yolks
2 teaspoons vanilla extract
9 ladyfingers, split
1 cup prepared whipped
topping (8 calories per
tablespoon)
Fresh or canned fruit slices

In small bowl, sprinkle gelatin over
cold water; set aside. In small saucepan,
stir together sugar and cocoa; gradually stir in skim milk. Beat egg yolks
slightly; add to saucepan. Cook over
medium heat, stirring constantly, until
mixture just begins to boil; remove
from heat. Stir in gelatin and vanilla.
Pour into medium bowl; refrigerate,
stirring occasionally, until mixture
mounds from a spoon. Carefully fold
whipped topping into chocolate mixture. Meanwhile, line sides and bottom of 1-quart straight-sided dish
with aluminum foil; arrange ladyfingers
firmly around sides and bottom. Pour
in chocolate mixture; cover. Refrigerate 4 hours or until firm. Carefully
unmold from dish; peel off foil. Slice;
serve with fresh fruit. *8 servings.*

Nutrition Information Per Serving:

Calories	280	Cholesterol, mg	55
Protein, gm	9	Sodium, mg	190
Carbohydrates, gm	52	Calcium, mg	125
Fat, gm	4		

*Top to Bottom: Choco-Lite Ladyfinger Dessert,
recipe page 90; Caribbean Freeze, recipe page 89;
Lighter Cocoa Cheesecake, recipe page 90.*

INDEX

A

Almond Chocolate Cookie Bars 81
Almond MINI CHIP Shortbread 80
Almond Orange Dainties 62

B

Black Forest Mini Cheesecakes 49
Black Magic Cake 6
Brandied Chocolate Sauce 28
Brownies & Bars
Almond Chocolate Cookie Bars . . . 81
Almond MINI CHIP Shortbread 80
Cherry-Bright Chocolate Brownies . 74
Chippy Chewy Bars 80
Chocolate Chunk Raspberry Bars . . 82
Chocolate Cream Cheese Brownies . . 76
Cocoa Raisin-Nut Brownie Bars . . . 76
Creamy Filled Brownies 74
English Toffee Bars 83
Fudgey Chocolate Cookie Bars 83
HERSHEY'S Best Brownies 79
HERSHEY'S Premium Doubly
   Chocolate Brownies 77
Mississippi Mud Brownies 78
Peanut Butter Chip Brownies 77
Peanut Butter Marble Brownies . . . 78
Peanutty Chewy Bars 75
Rocky Road Brownies 79
Vanilla Chip Lemon Bars 80

C

Cakes
Black Magic Cake 6
Chocolate Bar Cake 6
Chocolate Chip Snack Cake 8
Chocolate Raspberry Pound Cake . . 15
Chocolate Truffle Cake Supreme . . . 14
Crater Cake 14
Dark Chocolate Pecan Torte 8
Double Chocolate Cocoa Cupcakes . . 12
Espresso Filled Mini Cakes 11
Feathery Fudge Cake 13
HERSHEY'S Disappearing Cake 13
Hot Fudge Pudding Cake 9
MINI CHIP Angel Cake 12
MINI CHIP Sour Cream Streusel Cake . 16
Montana Mountain Cake 17
Old-Fashioned Chocolate Cake 9
Triple Chocolate Torte 16

Candies & Snacks
Chocolate Nut Clusters 57
Chocolate Snack Blocks 58
Chocolate-Almond Fudge 53
Chocolate-Covered Almond Apricot
   Tassies 53
Chocolatey Peanut Brittle 55
Cocoa Nut Break-Up 57
Creamy Double Decker Fudge 56
Double Peanut Truffles 52
Peanutty Rocky Road 55
Rich Cocoa Fudge 52
Semi-Sweet Chocolate Fudge 56
Vanilla Chip Trail Mix 59
Vanilla-Covered Strawberries 58
Caribbean Freeze 89
Celebration Tarts 32
Cheesecakes
Black Forest Mini Cheesecakes . . . 49
Chocolate Almond Cheesecake . . . 42
Chocolate Cheesecake 44
Chocolate Chip Pumpkin
   Cheesecake 42
Chocolate Drizzled Peanut Butter
   Cheesecake 43
Chocolate Ribbon Cheesecake . . . 47
Easy No-Bake Peanut Butter
   Cheesecake 48
Neapolitan Cheesecake 46
Paisley Print Cheesecake 44
Raspberry Chocolate Swirl
   Cheesecake 45
Cherry-Bright Chocolate Brownies . . 74
Chippy Chewy Bars 80
Choco-Berry Bavarian Cream 22
Choco-Berry Freeze 27
Chocolate Almond Biscotti 63
Chocolate Almond Cheesecake . . . 42
Chocolate Bar Cake 6
Chocolate Cheesecake 44
Chocolate Chip Pumpkin Cheesecake . 42
Chocolate Chip Snack Cake 8
Chocolate Chunk Blondies 67
Chocolate Chunk Raspberry Bars . . . 82
Chocolate Clouds 64
Chocolate Cream Cheese Brownies . . 76
Chocolate Cream Cheese Frosting . . . 19
Chocolate Drizzled Peanut Butter
   Cheesecake 43
Chocolate Glaze 18
Chocolate Marble Cheesepie 32
Chocolate Mousse and Praline Pie . . 37
Chocolate Nut Clusters 57
Chocolate Oatmeal Cookies 70

Chocolate Raspberry Pound Cake . . 15
Chocolate Ribbon Cheesecake 47
Chocolate Rum Mousse Pie 35
Chocolate Snack Blocks 58
Chocolate Truffle Cake Supreme 14
Chocolate Walnut Pie 34
Chocolate Yogurt Creme Pudding . . . 87
Chocolate-Almond Fudge 53
Chocolate-Banana Freeze 27
Chocolate-Covered Almond
    Apricot Tassies 53
Chocolate-Filled Meringue Shells
    with Strawberry Sauce 87
Chocolatey Peanut Brittle 55
Choco-Lite Ladyfinger Dessert 90
Choco-Orange Fluff 88
Cocoa Creme with Apricot Sauce . . . 29
Cocoa KISS Cookies 65
Cocoa Nut Break-up 57
Cocoa Oatmeal Treats 66
Cocoa Raisin-Nut Brownie Bars 76

Cookies
Almond Orange Dainties 62
Chocolate Almond Biscotti 63
Chocolate Chunk Blondies 67
Chocolate Clouds 64
Chocolate Oatmeal Cookies 70
Cocoa KISS Cookies 65
Cocoa Oatmeal Treats 66
HERSHEY'S Great American
    Chocolate Chip Cookies 64
Oatmeal Brownie Drops 65
Peanut Butter Crisps 68
Pecan-Topped Chocolate Cookies . 71
Peppermint Pattie Cookies 69
Pineapple and Vanilla Chip Drops . . 69
REESE'S Chewy Chocolate Cookies . 66
REESE'S Peanut Blossoms 71
Scrumptious Chocolate Fruit and
    Nut Cookies 68
Tropical Nut Crisps 66
Crater Cake 14
Creamy Double Decker Fudge 56
Creamy Filled Brownies 74

D
Dark Chocolate Pecan Torte 8
Desserts
Brandied Chocolate Sauce 28
Choco-Berry Bavarian Cream 22
Choco-Berry Freeze 27
Chocolate-Banana Freeze 27
Cocoa Creme with Apricot Sauce . . 29
Fudgey Chocolate Cherry Cups . . . 29
Milk Chocolate Pots de Crème . . . 23
Mocha-Filled Cream Puffs 24
Orange-Chocolate Mousse 23
Peanut Butter Washington Squares . 26

Pears with Chocolate-Orange Sauce . 22
Vanilla Chip Fruit Tart 24
Double Chocolate Cocoa Cupcakes . . 12
Double Peanut Truffles 52

E
Easy No-Bake Peanut Butter
    Cheesecake 48
English Toffee Bars 83
Espresso Filled Mini Cakes 11

F
Feathery Fudge Cake 13
Festive Frozen Peanut Butter
    Pecan Pie 34
Frostings
Chocolate Cream Cheese Frosting . . 19
Chocolate Glaze 18
HERSHEY'S Chocolate Frosting 18
Lemony Vanilla Milk Chip Frosting . . 19
One-Bowl Buttercream Frosting . . . 18
Quick Chocolate Fudge Frosting . . . 18
Fruit-Filled Chocolate Dreams 88
Fudgey Chocolate Cherry Cups 29
Fudgey Chocolate Cookie Bars 83

H
HERSHEY'S Best Brownies 79
HERSHEY'S Chocolate Frosting 18
HERSHEY'S Disappearing Cake 13
HERSHEY'S Great American
    Chocolate Chip Cookies 64
HERSHEY'S Premium Doubly
    Chocolate Brownies 77
Hot Fudge Pudding Cake 9

I
Innkeeper Pie 36

L
Lemony Vanilla Milk Chip Frosting . . 19
Lighter Cocoa Cheesecake 90
Lighter Desserts
Caribbean Freeze 89
Chocolate Yogurt Creme Pudding . . 87
Chocolate-Filled Meringue Shells
    with Strawberry Sauce 87
Choco-Lite Ladyfinger Dessert 90
Choco-Orange Fluff 88
Fruit-Filled Chocolate Dreams 88
Lighter Cocoa Cheesecake 90
Lighter Than Air Chocolate
    Almond Parfaits 89

M

Milk Chocolate Pots de Crème 23
MINI CHIP Angel Cake 12
MINI CHIP Sour Cream Streusel Cake . . 16
Mississippi Mud Brownies 78
Mocha Bavarian Pie 39
Mocha-Filled Cream Puffs 24
Montana Mountain Cake 17

N

Neapolitan Cheesecake 46

O

Oatmeal Brownie Drops 65
Old-Fashioned Chocolate Cake 9
One-Bowl Buttercream Frosting 18
Orange-Chocolate Mousse 23

P

Paisley Print Cheesecake 44
Peanut Butter Chip Brownies 77
Peanut Butter Crisps 68
Peanut Butter Marble Brownies . . . 78
Peanut Butter Washington Squares . . 26
Peanutty Chewy Bars 75
Peanutty Rocky Road 55
Pears with Chocolate-Orange Sauce . . 22
Pecan-Topped Chocolate Cookies . . . 71
Peppermint Pattie Cookies 69
Pies
  Celebration Tarts 32
  Chocolate Marble Cheesepie 32
  Chocolate Mousse and Praline Pie . . 37
  Chocolate Rum Mousse Pie 35
  Chocolate Walnut Pie 34
  Festive Frozen Peanut Butter
    Pecan Pie 34
  Innkeeper Pie 36
  Mocha Bavarian Pie 39
  Three-In-One Chocolate Pudding
    & Pie Filling 38
  Triple Decker Chocolate Coconut
    Cream Pie 38
Pineapple and Vanilla Chip Drops 69

Q

Quick Chocolate Fudge Frosting 18

R

Raspberry Chocolate Swirl
  Cheesecake 45
REESE'S Chewy Chocolate Cookies . . 66
REESE'S Peanut Blossoms 71
Rich Cocoa Fudge 52
Rocky Road Brownies 79

S

Scrumptious Chocolate Fruit and
  Nut Cookies 68
Semi-Sweet Chocolate Fudge 56

T

Three-In-One Chocolate
  Pudding & Pie Filling 38
Triple Chocolate Torte 16
Triple Decker Chocolate Coconut
  Cream Pie 38
Tropical Nut Crisps 66

V

Vanilla Chip Fruit Tart 24
Vanilla Chip Lemon Bars 80
Vanilla Chip Trail Mix 59
Vanilla-Covered Strawberries 58